FINANCIAL ARMAGEDDON

PROTECTING YOUR FUTURE FROM

FOUR IMPENDING CATASTROPHES

MICHAEL J. PANZNER

 PUBLISHING

This publication is designed to provide accurate and authoritative information in regard to the subject matter covered. It is sold with the understanding that neither the author nor the publisher is engaged in rendering legal, accounting, or other professional service. If legal advice or other expert assistance is required, the services of a competent professional should be sought. The opinions expressed are those of the author and do not necessarily reflect the views of any other individual or organization.

Executive Editor: Jennifer Farthing
Development Editor: Joshua Martino
Production Editor: Karen Goodfriend
Production Artist: John Christensen
Cover Designer: Jody Billert, Design Literate

Published by Kaplan Publishing, a division of Kaplan, Inc.
888 Seventh Ave.
New York, NY 10106

Printed in the United States of America

07 08 09   10 9 8 7 6 5 4 3 2 1

Library of Congress Cataloging-in-Publication Data

Panzner, Michael J.
  Financial armageddon : protecting your future from four impending catastrophes / Michael J. Panzner.
p. cm.
ISBN-13: 978-1-4195-9608-7
ISBN-10: 1-4195-9608-X
1. Finance, Personal. 2. Investments. I. Title.
HG179.P196 2007
332.024–dc22
2006034506

For information about ordering Kaplan Publishing books at special quantity discounts, please call 1-800-KAP-ITEM or write to Kaplan Publishing, 888 Seventh Ave., 22nd Floor, New York, NY, 10106.

C o n t e n t s

PART THREE
FALLOUT

PART FOUR
DEFENSES

DEDICATION

To Catherine,
for all you do
and everything you are

Writing is something of a paradox; it is a solitary passion, yet its success invariably depends on the insights, support, hard work, and enthusiasm of other people. In that regard, I'd especially like to thank the following individuals: Bill Siegel for his enduring friendship, valuable editing assistance, and unwavering support for all these years; my brother Max for his creative energies, cutting-edge perspective, and questions that always force me to think; my sister Paige for her inspiring visions of success and infectious enthusiasm; my agent, John Willig, for his persistent belief in the project—and in me; Cynthia Zigmund, one of the first to see what needed to be heard; and Maureen McMahon, Jennifer Farthing, Joshua Martino, and Karen Goodfriend of Kaplan, who helped turn a rough vision into a polished reality.

Once again, I could not have gotten through this effort at all without the love, support, and understanding of my children, Sophie, Emily, Mollie, and Nellie, and my wife, Catherine, who really do make it all worthwhile.

Our world is a riskier place than it used to be. Whether from escalating conflict in the Mideast, rogue nations brandishing nuclear weapons, random attacks against innocent civilians, ruinous natural disasters, the emergence of global pandemics, or the fallout from volatile energy prices, we are increasingly vulnerable to a host of threats. Most Americans seem aware of these dangers, if only cursorily. We are familiar with war, diseases, and earthquakes. We understand that certain groups seek to subjugate others militarily or economically. We recognize that many individuals despise our country and wish to destroy everything for which we stand.

We know enough to be concerned about these risks and remain on the lookout for any signs of danger. We also realize that we may one day need to take action to protect ourselves and our loved ones.

But that is not the case with the devastating economic cataclysm that lies ahead.

Lacking the most primitive early-warning signal available to miners, we have no "canary in the coal mine" to raise the alarm over the broad-scale dangers of a toxic confluence of debt, derivatives, government guarantees, and unfunded retirement obligations.

There have indeed been voices in the wilderness warning of the dangers, but most have only highlighted certain aspects of this disturbingly vast labyrinth. The majority of Americans have blithely assumed that with rules, regulations, and capital cushions in place, as well as our long history of muddling through difficult times, there is no real cause for concern. Yet when it all starts to go wrong, and the supposedly unimaginable evolves into a horrifying reality, it will be too late to react. It will then be clear that these four developments have formed an explosive mix that is too unwieldy, too complex, and too rife with conflicts of interest for any individual or organization to come to grips with. As with deadly carbon monoxide spreading quickly and insidiously in the depths of a mine, many will find themselves overcome with financial ruin before they know what hit them.

Financial Armageddon: Protecting Your Future from Four Impending Catastrophes is a layperson's guide to four threats and the far-reaching impact they are poised to have on our lifestyles, our economy, and our society. The first is a burgeoning tower of public and private debt wobbling precariously on a foundation of greed, overindulgence, and fraud. The second is a multitrillion-dollar house of cards to which all Americans are exposed, though few of us know it. The third is a vast array of largely hidden promises that will ultimately remain unkept. The last is a retirement mirage that will leave millions cast adrift or financially enslaved until the day they die. Each is a ticking time bomb—all ready to explode at once.

A book on these threats has not yet been written for a few reasons. Many potential authors who are otherwise up to the task lack a solid understanding of the big-picture risks associated with modern day financial products, relationships, and markets. Moreover, the vast majority of those who are aware of the problems are bankers, Wall Street operators, and industry insiders who do not wish to kill the golden goose of profitability. Or they have decided to adopt an ostrich-like professional posture about the systemic dangers, despite their personal misgivings.

With time running out, a tragedy is in the making, and every American must acknowledge, understand, and prepare for it—before it is too late.

"Disasters never come alone."

—Chinese proverb

When the unraveling is fully under way, there will be a flood of lurid headlines. Amid the avalanche of hearings, lawsuits, arrests, and trials, stories about violent strikes and protests will vie with news of plunging markets and businesses going belly up. Every day, tales of foreclosures and broken lives will blanket the airwaves. Many financial institutions will shut their doors, often with little warning. Rumor-filled bank runs will be commonplace. Finger-pointing will also be widespread, as politicians, regulators, and corporate chiefs scramble for cover in the face of increasingly hostile public opinion.

Meanwhile, Americans will scratch their heads and wonder how it all went so wrong so fast, or why they had not been aware of the dangers before. In reality, we should have seen it coming. Signs of impending doom were everywhere, plain for all to see, in the years leading up to the wide-ranging meltdown. Still, even if people had been aware of the gravity of the situation, it seemed that few cared all that much.

That certainly appeared to be the case when President George W. Bush and the Republican-controlled Congress, in a charade of sober concern, agreed to boost the federal borrowing limit to $9 trillion in the spring of 2006. This was an extraordinary increase of more than 50 percent from five years earlier. It was another regrettable, but now unavoidable, step to fund the latest in a long string of understated multibillion-dollar deficits.

Apathy was also in the air when the U.S. personal savings rate went negative for the first time since the Great Depression and total household debt exceeded 150 percent of disposable income. American consumers were not only spending what they earned but also a great deal of what they didn't. And few noticed an April 2006 survey by Phoenix Management suggesting that two-thirds of U.S. lenders thought the country was in the middle of a real estate bubble, and half of them believed the bubble was about to burst—or already had.

Most Americans did not worry when the nation's top auditor, Comptroller General David Walker, suggested that the United States could be likened to Rome before the fall. Or when he said that the nation was facing "a demographic tsunami" that "will never recede." Even more surprising was the muted reaction to an article written by Boston University economics professor Laurence J. Kotlikoff for the July/August 2006 Federal Reserve Bank of St. Louis *Review*. He asked—rhetorically, it would seem—"Is the United States Bankrupt?"

After an initial flurry of concern, people also glossed over Warren Buffett's warnings about derivatives, which he characterized as "financial weapons of mass destruction." Yet he would eventually seem prescient after he wrote in Berkshire Hathaway's 2002 annual report that "[t]hese instruments will almost certainly multiply in variety and number until some event makes their toxicity clear."

Few paid attention to warnings from Eric Breval, the head of the $15.5 billion Swiss state pension fund, in a November 2005 Bloomberg report. He discussed plans to shift assets away from the United States and referred to the financial "time bomb" that the nation's largest mortgage lenders, Fannie Mae and Freddie

Mac, were sitting on. The same held true in April 2006, when Citigroup vice chairman William Rhodes told the *Wall Street Journal,* "We are in a situation similar to that which existed in the spring of 1997, when threats existed to market stability and a lot of people didn't want to see it."

Perhaps that's it: Americans just didn't want to know. Or maybe they actually didn't see anything wrong or out of the ordinary. Everywhere you looked, policymakers, politicians, and pundits insisted that the financial system and the so-called Goldilocks economy were alive and well, and there was no reason for anyone to believe otherwise.

Then again, perhaps it was just too easy to believe the fairy tale that the good times could last forever.

To be sure, only scant evidence existed in early 2006 that the average Joe had put the brakes on spending, despite increasingly burdensome levels of borrowing and the fact that real—inflation-adjusted—wages had been stagnant for years. "Why call it quits now?" consumers argued. Indeed, Americans had carried on with their profligate ways far longer than many observers had expected. This was partly because consumerism had become an end in itself. It was a new religion—a new American dream supported by an endless stream of advertiser-supported media.

Almost everyone was imbued with a get-it-now, live-for-today perspective, a kind of financial hedonism enabled and repeatedly overstimulated by an aggressively competitive, rapidly innovating, but ultimately self-serving financial services sector. To that end, lenders and borrowers joined hands and helped create a massive real estate and mortgage market bubble, allowing consumers to "extract," as the euphemism went, $2.5 trillion in debt-financed equity from their homes from 2001 through 2005.

There was a growing sense of entitlement, especially among the 78 million baby boomers—Americans born between 1946 and 1965—as well as a widespread desire for wealth without work. For many, engaging in excessive borrowing, self-deception, and a rejiggering of priorities to support a lifestyle they felt they needed and deserved was just the way life was. A quick read of history suggests this delusion is common among the citizenry of fading and failed empires.

Perhaps it wasn't so odd, because almost everyone agreed on the script, that few gave clear thought to the dangerous indulgences and unsustainable financial imbalances that had built up over the years.

Of course, it didn't help that many factors that spawned the multifaceted disaster seemed too complicated and far-reaching for most people to comprehend. Without the benefit of sophisticated financial wisdom, the majority saw the various influences as unrelated to each other. Moreover, few Americans understood how and to what degree globalization, consolidation, innovation, and technology had altered the financial landscape. It was also hard to grasp the paradoxical idea that long periods of stability, which many viewed as inherently positive, were actually destabilizing. As economist Hyman Minsky once noted, the good times tended to foster the complacency and risky behavior that lay the groundwork for upheaval.

Even those who sensed early on that the end was near might not have grasped the significance of certain developments, like changes in state and local government accounting rules for post-employment health care and other nonpension benefits. First implemented by the Government Accounting Standards Board in 2006, these rules were seen as a way to ensure that municipal finances were more transparent than in the past. The new requirements were meant to hold politicians accountable for at least some of their "free lunch" promises.

It seemed like a great idea. But as with several other rules and reforms that came into play up to and after the stock market bubble burst, they would ultimately have unintended—and unwelcome— consequences. In this case, the scale of once-hidden promises to current and former workers would turn out to be $1 trillion dollars, according to an expert cited by the *New York Times*. Eventually, that revelation will spur widespread credit downgrades, leave many municipalities cut off from financing, force drastic budget cuts, and trigger an ultimately unsustainable push for higher taxes that will only add to the fallout from other catastrophes, including a rapidly deflating credit bubble, a systemic financial crisis, a collapsing economy, and an imploding derivatives market.

By then, the dangers that a few observers had foreseen—which were discounted, misunderstood, or overlooked—will be the only thing that growing numbers of Americans will be able to think about.

Part One

THREATS

1

DEBT

"A billion here, a billion there, and pretty soon you're talking real money."
—**Senator Everett Dirksen**

Sometime during 2007 or 2008, the flickering display on the national debt clock will almost certainly run out of room. The ever-increasing figure will not be able to fit the extra digit that will pop up when federal government borrowing breaks the $10 trillion dollar barrier. Unless, of course, the Durst family, who owns the clock in New York's Times Square, decides to upgrade it or there is a sudden bout of fiscal responsibility in Washington.

Unfortunately, the odds of the latter are almost certainly nil.

More likely is that the United States will soon suffer the fallout of the live-for-today orgy of borrowing and extravagance that has already foisted an untenable economic and financial burden on future generations. Americans will also confront the daunting impact of what Albert Einstein once described as "the greatest mathematical discovery of all time": the compounding of interest.

Barring major spending cuts or tax hikes, the combination of higher interest rates, the costly war in Iraq, and various other forms of public sector profligacy could help boost the national debt by another $3 trillion by 2010, according to experts cited by *USA To-*

day in November 2005 And that figure does not even take into account other obligations, such as Social Security and Medicare.

Like individuals and companies, governments have often relied on debt to make up for shortfalls when current income is lacking. Indeed, during more prudent times, borrowing is one of many valid financial strategies to acquire productive assets, which can generate decent returns and repay principal and interest down the road. Borrowed money can also make it easier to finance expensive but necessary projects or acquisitions, such as a public sewer system, a company warehouse, or a place to live, when upfront costs can't be met with current resources. Even then, the amount of debt any individual or entity might take on has traditionally been constrained by old-fashioned prudence and a grown-up sense of responsibility.

But this dynamic has changed in the last few decades.

The Federal Reserve, whose stated mission is to ensure price stability, seemed to adopt a new mind-set during the 18-year tenure of Alan Greenspan, former chairman of the Federal Reserve, that was predicated on cutting rates at the drop of a hat and using monetary policy to try to eliminate normal cyclical downswings in the economy. Like force-feeding a duck to make foie gras, the Greenspan-led Fed appeared determined to stuff the U.S. economy with enough borrowed money to ensure that something of value was created—even if in the end it killed the bird.

In addition, the upbeat mood of the 1980s and the heady, go-go days of the 1990s convinced many Americans that circumstances would invariably get better, no matter what hiccups came up along the way. The United States had not seen a bone-jarring, consumer-led recession for 15 years, and one could argue that the optimism was justified. Why prepare for the worst by saving more or borrowing less if the occasional downdraft is unlikely to last long? Ever-growing investment returns, an endless housing boom, and the Federal Reserve had conditioned Americans to believe that, inevitable good fortune would eventually bail them out—should it even prove necessary.

The financial system had also undergone revolutionary change, both in attitudes about credit and in the way the lending process worked. Technological innovation increased efficiency and facilitated financial institutions' offering people all sorts of products and services not previously available to them. Advanced communications, quantum leaps in computing capabilities, and the power and reach of the Internet enabled anyone to borrow money for almost any purpose. The same developments also made it easier than ever to seek out and tap those with funds to spare.

Modern financial engineering had also altered the prudent lending relationships that were a hallmark of days gone by. Bankers no longer relied upon getting to know their customers or on experience-driven gut instinct to assess a borrower's willingness and ability to repay a loan. Instead, they used technology and credit "scoring" methods—FICO® being the most common—that are based on prior payment history and other seemingly relevant factors of future creditworthiness. Or else they simply looked at the collateral involved—regardless of a debtor's ability to pay.

The same seemed to hold true for many who invested in fixed-income securities. If a bond had an appropriate credit rating from an agency like Moody's, or if it was guaranteed by Fannie Mae or an insurer like MBIA, or if it was secured in some way, then it was worth owning, despite other considerations that once might have raised red flags.

And when it came to the U.S. government, few Americans contemplated the possibility of default when shelling out for Treasury bills or bonds. To use an old cliché, most people assumed that their money was "as safe as houses," which is ironic given the havoc a bursting real estate bubble will eventually wreak on government finances. Yet in decades past, investors might have balked at financing the debt of a nation with a current account balance—the difference between what it consumes and what it produces—of close to 7 percent of output, as well as other obligations that seemed to grow exponentially. Even investors outside our borders, who should have known better, were oblivious to the realities of an American economy gone bad. By 2006, foreigners owned over 42 percent of outstanding Treasury securities, up from 30 percent only six years earlier.

Unlike boring, old-fogy bankers, those putting up the money didn't seem to have the same degree of concern about whether they would get back their principal.

Part of their reasoning undoubtedly came down to securitization—a process whereby loans or other assets are lumped together and essentially resold, with the payments from debtors often sliced into many pieces with different coupons, maturity dates, and risk parameters to suit the multifaceted needs of various end investors.

In a simple example, XYZ Bank convinces prospective home buyers to arrange their mortgages through the lender. Once the paperwork is complete and the funds paid out, the bank sells the newly created loans to a "special-purpose vehicle," or SPV, for the face value plus a fee. At the same time, investment bankers arrange to have these SPVs issue debt—in much the same way an established company might—that could then be sold to institutional fixed-income money managers, such as pension or mutual funds, or even directly to retail investors.

The mortgage-backed securities, or MBSs, would usually be comprised of several classes, or "tranches," with the higher-rated securities having first dibs on the proceeds flowing into the SPV from the mortgage-paying homeowners. The riskier tranches would, however, be designated for a larger share of the interest received than would the more stable variety. Typically, the lower-rated tranches would be structured in such a way that they would be the first to suffer losses if some of the homeowners whose loans were in the "pool" defaulted on their mortgages. By tradition, the riskiest slice is called the "equity tranche." The yield for each tranche would vary, with the overall average working out to less than what the underlying mortgagees were paying. The difference would go to cover the fees of those involved in the securitization and later sale to investors, as well as any legal and administrative costs. Anything left over after making good on loan losses would go to the equity tranche holders.

In the end, the bank would be back where it started—albeit with a quick profit on its original loans—ready to originate another round of new debts and add to the total amount of credit outstanding. Meanwhile, investors would hand over cash to purchase the mortgage-backed securities issued by the SPV and would receive interest payments in return. Eventually, as the underlying mortgages were paid off, the proceeds would flow back to the MBS owners as principal.

And everyone, it seems, would be happy. This is most likely why more than half of all U.S. residential mortgages were incorporated in mortgage-backed securities by 2006, according to the Bank for International Settlements.

Of course, the assumption is that most homeowners whose loans are in a pool will actually make their payments on time—and will eventually repay all of the original principal. This belief will prove fanciful in the wake of a bursting property bubble and an economy that abruptly flips from modest growth to sharp contraction. All of a sudden, large numbers of believers in the American dream will find themselves out of a job, owing more on their homes than their properties are worth, or both. At that point, homeowners will either be unwilling or unable to hand over what they owe.

Making matters worse are the many other obligations that Americans acquired during the credit-bubble years. Of course, the scale of exposure will not have seemed quite as daunting as it will when everything goes wrong. By then, however, the straitjacket of debt will prove to have an extraordinary impact on every aspect of economic life.

Still, economic catastrophe should not be such a rude awakening. Anyone could have anticipated that our attitudes about debt, the widespread availability of borrowed money, and low U.S. interest rates would encourage Americans to borrow first and ask questions later. It was so easy, in fact, that the ratio of total debt to gross domestic product, a measure of U.S. economic output, rose to more than 300 percent by 2005, exceeding the record of 290 percent last seen just prior to the 1929 stock market crash. And net external debt, which measures the difference between what we owe the rest of the world and their obligations to us, reached more than $3 trillion, having been a surplus only a few years before.

According to the Federal Reserve's triennial "Survey of Consumer Finances," more than three-quarters of American families owed money in 2004, while the overall debt load of borrowers surged by 33.9 percent in a three-year span. The spree continued in 2005, as household debt rose 12 percent, the fastest rate in 20 years. It wasn't just that the percentages were large; the raw numbers were also mind-boggling, with the tally adding up to over $8.8 trillion in mortgage debt, $2 trillion of consumer debt, and a cool trillion in home equity loans and second mortgages.

Borrowing money was fast becoming the bad habit of choice for American consumers, many of whom were finding it hard to "just say no" or were oblivious to the longer-term consequences of boosting debt exposure to hitherto unseen levels. Households spent a record 13.75 percent of their after-tax income on servicing required interest and principal payments during the last quarter of 2005.

Americans borrowed so carelessly because they focused only on the payments involved. When it came to obtaining financing, the number that always stood out was the monthly carrying charge, or "nut." That amount was usually highlighted in big, bold letters, unlike other important details, such as the total that was owed, including interest, or the penalties that would accrue if the loan was not paid on time.

Automakers had long relied on this strategy to get buyers to sign on the dotted line. Yet when higher rates made it difficult to offer monthly terms that were palatable, Ford, General Motors, and others would eventually extend the maturity dates of the agreements by 50 percent or more. Or they would push leases where, in essence, monthly payments covered only the interest and part of the principal—in exchange for 0 percent of the ownership. In

March 2005, for instance, Edmunds.com reported that 19.8 percent of all vehicles were leased rather than bought, the highest rate since 2001.

In fact, a variety of intermediaries did all they could to ensure that even those who lacked the financial wherewithal got their share of borrowed money, especially when it came to property-based lending. In the spring of 2005, reports indicated that around 10 percent of homeowners had zero-to-negative equity in their homes whereas nearly 30 percent of buyers had none. That figure was not surprising given how easy it had become to acquire a property with no money down.

Another way around the problem was to dilute underwriting standards or make the terms more "affordable," especially for buyers with spotty credit records or income that was hard to prove on paper. Many of these "subprime" borrowers discovered that by taking on adjustable-rate mortgages, or ARMs, which featured ultralow introductory rates instead of the traditional 30-year, fixed-rate loans, they could tap into the American dream and own their own home. Some had to stretch even harder than that, but bankers were only too willing to oblige. They began offering other nontraditional products, including interest-only loans, with the entire principal payable at the end of the term, and payment option ARMs, whereby borrowers had the choice of remitting less than the interest and principal due in any given month.

Unfortunately, this kind of affordability had a downside known as "negative amortization," which leaves many "owners" owing more on their property than they did when they initially purchased it. They would then be, to use the vernacular of the industry, "upside down." Many also didn't quite realize that having adjustable mortgages meant just that—that their rates and payments could go up, perhaps by a lot. According to a 2006 Fed study, 41 percent of homeowners with ARMs didn't have any idea about the maximum interest rate that they could be charged.

But the risks didn't seem to matter. By 2005, 13.4 percent of outstanding mortgages were classified as subprime, up from 2.1

percent in 1999, according to the Mortgage Bankers Association. In addition, half of the mortgages underwritten in 2005 and 2006 were ARMs, while nearly 10 million mortgages—a quarter of the total outstanding—carried adjustable interest rates. And during 2006 and 2007, up to $2.5 trillion of those loans would be "reset," meaning payments would spike from their initial low levels after more than two years of interest rate hikes by the Federal Reserve.

It was going to be ugly, that's for sure.

Not all of the borrowing was for the purchase of new homes. According to the National Association of Realtors, a record 39.9 percent of the properties that Americans bought in 2005 were for vacation or investment, with many owners counting on a buoyant rental market and continually rising prices to keep the juggling act going. Regardless of the reasoning behind the purchases, house prices had outstripped income growth by a factor of six over five years, according to a Harvard University study, helping to create an unsustainable real estate bubble of epic proportions.

Property-related borrowing also played other roles in the economy. Refinancing activity that tapped home equity—the value of property less any debt owed on it—grew to represent a sizable slice of the overall market. Enabled by surging home prices and heavily marketed by banks and other lenders as an alternative to unsecured but high-rate credit cards, "cash-out refis" became an increasingly popular way to raise funds for property owners—and even some prospective purchasers who didn't have quite enough money for a required down payment.

The numbers turned out to be huge. From 2001 through 2005, the sum total of mortgage equity withdrawals, or MEWs, was estimated to be around $2.5 trillion, according to the *Weekly Standard*. Some analysts suggested, in fact, that MEWs may have accounted for a substantial share of U.S. economic growth over the five-year period.

Along with the direct economic impact, however, developments in the credit markets dramatically altered the distribution and structure of interest rate and default risk in the American financial system. For a start, with the gradual move from unsecured towards secured lending, debtors assumed a greater financial burden in the event that they could not pay their bills. Although a substantial proportion of assets has traditionally been available to pay off creditors following a filing for bankruptcy, debtors once had been able to "affirm"—agree to keep paying—secured debts to shield at least some of their equity interest from credit card and other unsecured lenders. Many states also allowed certain property, including homes, to be excluded from the pool of assets that could be used to satisfy existing creditors.

The shift toward variable-rate debt has also altered the impact of a change in yields. In the past, bankers' bottom lines tended to be adversely affected when interest rates moved higher. But with adjustable-rate mortgages and the like accounting for a significantly larger share of a market that comprises 45 percent of total nonfinancial debt, borrowers—individual Americans—will increasingly feel the heat. It is not just the mortgage market that has been affected. According to Bankrate.com, by early 2006, approximately two-thirds of all credit cards carried variable interest rates, a noticeable increase from the 55 percent level only 12 months earlier.

As lenders aggressively courted business with an almost singular focus on generating fees and turnover, many invariably acted foolishly. The Federal Bureau of Investigation, for example, estimated that lenders had been ripped off to the tune of $1 billion in mortgage-related fraud in 2005 alone. Still, there were plenty of willing participants in the ever-expanding credit bubble, many of whom already found themselves under the gun even before things began to unravel. By 2005, for example, there were more than two million bankruptcies, up from 616,000 in 1989, though the surge was certainly abetted by a rush to file ahead of October's implementation of the extremely debtor-unfriendly Bankruptcy Abuse Prevention and Consumer Protection Act.

Homeowners and consumers were not the only ones who leveraged up—corporate America did the same, though many businesses were also benefiting from what Bill Gross, chairman of bond fund powerhouse PIMCO, called the "finance-based economy." During 2005, gross issuance of international bonds and notes by U.S. entities rose by 8 percent to $836 billion, while net issuance increased almost threefold to $114 billion, according to the Bank for International Settlements. In contrast, reported *The Economist*, the profits of financial firms in America had risen from 4 percent of the overall total to more than 40 percent since 1982, with the industry accounting for almost 25 percent of total stock market capitalization.

The corporate side also benefited from the frantic urge to boost volume that was rippling through the consumer lending market, with creditors falling over themselves to offer overly generous terms and conditions. In April 2006, for example, the *Wall Street Journal* reported that lenders were mandating fewer covenants—performance hurdles—for business borrowers to clear. Such accommodation helped boost the annual rate of growth of nonfinancial company borrowing to its fastest pace in five years.

Meanwhile, borrowing for speculation, investments, arbitrage, and corporate finance–related activity had been growing sharply as well. In sophisticated, lightly regulated, and often actively traded investment pools known as "hedge funds," assets under management, often boosted many times over through aggressive leverage, were estimated to have reached $1.5 trillion for the entire industry.

Activity was also surging in the "private equity" sector, which used large dollops of borrowed money to acquire what were deemed to be undervalued companies. During early 2006, according to *Forbes*, 2,700 funds were raising half a trillion dollars to invest, which could then "bankroll them for $2.5 trillion in deals, given their penchant for putting $4 (or more) of debt leverage atop every dollar they put in." Intense competition also forced many to lower their standards, with some evaluating and accepting deals on multiples of seven times EBIT—earnings before interest and taxes—versus multiples of four or five only a few years earlier.

Wall Street firms and traditional lenders, of course, were reaping the rewards of the borrowing boom, especially in the real estate sector. By 2005, mortgage-related activities accounted for a record 62 percent of commercial banks' earnings versus 33 percent in 1987. Financial institutions were heavily geared to the property market in other respects, too. In a spring 2005 speech addressing proposed commercial real estate (CRE) guidance by U.S. banking agencies, Susan Schmidt Bies, Federal Reserve governor, noted that average CRE exposure for certain midsized banks was near 300 percent of capital, a level double that of the late 1980s and early 1990s.

Still, when it came to playing the game of modern-day finance, few firms could match Fannie Mae and Freddie Mac in their use of leverage or their lopsidedly bullish exposure to the fortunes of the real estate market. Together, the two government-sponsored entities, or GSEs, held nearly $1.5 trillion in loans and mortgage-backed securities and guaranteed $2.4 trillion of MBSs owned by banks and other investors as of the first quarter of 2005. This created tremendous vulnerability in the financial system. Some banks, for example, had exposure to Fannie and Freddie securities amounting to more than 100 percent of their capital.

In the public sector, it was not only the federal government and the GSEs that were on a borrowing spree. During 2005, issuance of new state and local bonds hit an all-time high of $405 billion, up 13 percent from 2004, with more than $2 trillion worth outstanding. Indeed, the amount of debt raised in the capital markets in recent years has been staggering. The Bond Market Association, an industry trade group, reported that overall U.S. bond issuance reached $5.52 trillion in 2005, led by a record-setting $1.1 trillion for asset-backed securities such as MBSs.

The problem with all of this borrowing, of course, is that much of it was taken on in the hope that the economy, borrower income levels, or the assets that backed many of the debts would be sufficient to secure repayment. This assumption, as it turns out, will prove seriously flawed.

2

THE RETIREMENT
SYSTEM

"Sooner or later everyone sits down to a banquet of consequences."
—**Robert Louis Stevenson**

By the time all the numbers
are tallied and reported, at least some people will paraphrase
Shakespeare. They will suggest, with more than a hint of serious-
ness, that it's time to "kill all the accountants."

But those numerate types with the green eye shades won't be
to blame. Rather, it will be leaders of the public and private sectors
who put off an accurate assessment of what the future held, even
though they knew a day of reckoning would come. When promises worth trillions of dollars made by American chief executives,
state and local officials, and politicians in Washington are finally
brought to light, figuring out how to pay for them all or, more
realistically, how much should be paid will be a truly Herculean
task.

Certainly no small number of leaders and policymakers were
somewhat aware that a difficult future beckoned. Most private
pensions were governed by reporting guidelines and other requirements established under the Employee Retirement Income
Security Act of 1974, or ERISA, meaning that a few concerns had
already seeped into the open. Moreover, some shortcomings of

the federally administered social safety net had been at least partly addressed by the introduction in 1982 of a new payroll tax following concerns raised by the National Commission on Social Security Reform about the system's going broke.

But few Americans are knowledgeable about the absolute scale of their long-run financial exposure, largely because of the way retirement-related promises had—legally, in most cases—been accounted for in the past.

Historically, pension and other postemployment benefits, or OPEBs, including medical coverage for retired workers, have barely been acknowledged. Risks and liabilities were frequently buried deep in footnotes or in hard-to-decipher reports and were not ordinarily listed as line items in financial statements. Aside from being "off balance sheet," many of the liabilities were obscured through the use of nebulous accounting practices and unrealistic assumptions about future interest rates, investment returns, and health care inflation. Another problem with the vast majority of OPEBs is that they were accounted for on a pay-as-you-go basis, where only current-year program revenues and expenses were recorded. That made it difficult to grasp the full extent of what is referred to as the "benefits gap," or the difference between the present value of what had been promised versus what had been set aside.

But in the post-Enron era, there is a growing emphasis on illuminating what was once obscured. That view took on greater urgency with the prospect that poor investment returns following the collapse of the 1990s stock market bubble might add to existing shortfalls.

At the municipal level, where a history of financial opacity and a never-ending series of blue-sky promises have been the norm, the need for change was obvious. For politicians who often measure careers in two- or four-year cycles, trading "free" promises involving pensions and other long-term benefits to unionized public sector workers in exchange for lower but politically palatable pay increases was usually too good an opportunity to pass up.

When the Government Accounting Standards Board (GASB) amended its rules in 2004, however, it created a ticking time bomb. GASB 45 mandated that governments and agencies, in a staggered rollout beginning December 15, 2006, estimate the "actuarial liability" of their OPEBs—the net cost in current dollars—and the amortized equivalent over 30 years. Suddenly, decades of generous promises would be placed under a harsh light—and the results were not going to be pretty. Based on early estimates, the annual costs of postretirement health care benefits could turn out to be up to 20 times as large as expected. According to one expert cited by the *New York Times*, the tab for all state and local governments will be as much as $1 trillion.

Add to that more than $300 billion—or, according to Barclays Global Investors, $800 billion if more conservative private-sector accounting methods are used—of underfunded municipal pension plans. Nearly all of these plans are traditional defined-benefit schemes under which retirees are guaranteed a set payout for life and sponsors bear the investment and other risks.

In one fell swoop, the financial health of state and local government will have taken a gargantuan turn for the worse, and talk of a massive taxpayer bailout will fill the air. This will lay the groundwork for a firestorm that will only be made worse by a crumbling economy, unraveling financial markets, and fewer new workers replacing older ones. Already stretched precariously thin in many locales, municipal finances will come under relentless attack as state and local government authorities are forced to take such drastic steps as cutting spending, raising taxes, and attempting to borrow additional funds. The sum of these endeavors will come to naught.

While revelations about the financial position of state and local governments will be a growing cause for concern, an even greater threat will finally dawn on investors, foreigners, politicians, and individual Americans after years of largely ignored warnings: U.S. government finances are also in a complete shambles.

Much of the problem stems from a failure of leadership and the inherent flaws of a system where politicians must constantly curry favor with special interest groups. Still, the nation's demographic profile certainly made matters worse. Americans have been growing old quickly, and 78 million baby boomers will soon draw upon the wealth of younger Americans. People are living longer, too; the average life expectancy increased from 75.4 years in 1990 to an all-time high of 77.6 in 2005—two years in less than a generation. By 2030, twice as many people will be 65 or older as there are now. And by 2040, one out of every four Americans will be in that age bracket.

That means only one thing: barring any dramatic changes in benefits, the already large cost of the social safety net will expand rapidly. But our means to support it and the working-age population that underwrites it are not growing. In 1942, seven years after Social Security was first established, there were 42 workers for every beneficiary. By 2002, the ratio was down to 3.3, and by 2030, it is expected to drop by another 50 percent to 2.2.

Municipal finances will also feel the strain of an aging population. So will private-sector pension plans, especially in industries such as steel, autos, utilities, and airlines, which once employed hundreds of thousands of workers.

For many people, hardest to swallow will be the realization that American prosperity is no longer limitless. A number of safety-net commitments began when the United States and much of its industry were market leaders and world beaters. Back then, a majority of Americans accepted that the wealth of the nation should not only be shared with those who helped create it but also with those who were less fortunate. Before Medicare was established in 1965, for instance, many older Americans found it difficult to cover the cost of health care, and widespread sentiment held that society owed them more for their troubles. In recent years, however, actuaries have increasingly warned about the rapidly rising cost of entitlement programs, such as Social Security, Medicare, and Medicaid, the largesse of which have grown over time.

Undoubtedly, complacency has played a part. The United States has successfully weathered other so-called fiscal storms in the past. America thrived in the years leading up to 2006, even though we consumed far more than we produced and spent much more than we earned. But as the economic and financial tide turns, what had once fallen on deaf ears will almost certainly turn deafening—and investors, businesspeople, foreigners, and many others will grow increasingly fearful.

In 2006, University of Pennsylvania risk management professor Kent Smetters and Jagadeesh Gokhale of the Cato Institute estimated that, because of entitlement programs, the gap between projected federal spending and income might be as high as $65 trillion. Economist Laurence Kotlikoff puts the total of unfunded liabilities nearer to $80 trillion, over seven times the value of the gross domestic product (GDP), the nation's output of goods and services. To make up the difference, Smetters and Gokhale have warned that Social Security and Medicare payroll taxes would "need to double immediately," according to the *Christian Science Monitor*. The problems will grow even more intractable if health care spending exceeds the nearly 10 percent annual increases of recent decades, or if Washington adds other entitlement programs, such as the Medicare prescription benefit, which alone contributed more than $8 trillion to the total.

These numbers do not even take into account that Social Security has not been treated as the discrete "trust fund" many assume it to be. Rather, it has generally been viewed as just another taxpayer cash cow that could repeatedly be tapped by lawmakers in exchange for government IOUs that obscure the true state of the nation's budget morass. If Washington reported the finances of the United States using Generally Accepted Accounting Procedures—the methodology that public companies are required to use—instead of recording a $318 billion deficit in 2005, the federal budget gap would have been $3.5 trillion, or more than ten times as much, according to *USA Today*.

Hence, when the same newspaper noted that "[t]he nation could soon face its worst fiscal crisis since at least 1983, when Social Security bordered on bankruptcy," the federal entitlement system clearly had become a cancer, growing more dangerous with each passing year. Standard & Poor's warned, in the summer of 2006, that if current fiscal trends prevail, the U.S. sovereign credit rating could easily decline from AAA to A or BBB in the decade ahead.

Yet efforts at reform, including attempts by the George W. Bush administration to privatize Social Security, have gone nowhere. This failure partly reflects the reality that those who benefit from an all-encompassing social safety net are growing in numbers—and political clout.

Ironically, the retirement-related concerns in the private sector seem almost inconsequential in comparison. Nonetheless, they are another layer on an ever-growing fiscal disaster, a burden that must ultimately be paid for in one way or another. Like the public sector, corporate America has significant exposure to retiree health care costs. According to one estimate, two-thirds of the S&P 500 companies have some OPEB obligations, to the tune of about $300 billion—in addition to $150 billion of underfunding for employee pensions. At one company in particular, the numbers are indeed astonishing. As of early 2006, General Motors's unfunded pension promises were estimated to be as much as $31 billion—despite the company's claims to the contrary—while other postemployment benefits were thought to total more than twice as much, or $70 billion, according to some analysts.

Despite the similarities, there is a key difference between corporate America and the public sector when it comes to retirement-related liabilities. The private sector generally has more freedom to deal with future promises. It can alter the terms, either by watering down benefits or eliminating so-called perks like health care coverage for retirees. Companies can also "freeze" plans so that current employees cannot accrue any more benefits than they already have.

Many firms have shifted away from defined-benefit plans altogether in favor of others, such as 401(k) plans. Named after a section of the Internal Revenue Code and first introduced in 1979, 401(k) plans are a tax-deferred savings scheme that companies have readily adopted as a "defined-contribution" alternative to traditional pensions. Under such an arrangement, the amount of money paid into the plan, rather than the payouts at retirement, is fixed. In essence, investment, actuarial, and other risks are shifted from the sponsor—in most cases, the employer—to the employee.

As with the broad move to floating-rate borrowing fostered by mortgage and other lenders, the rise of 401(k) plans indicates that ordinary Americans have increasingly begun to shoulder risks traditionally assumed by businesses and governments. By cutting benefits and moving away from defined-pension arrangements, a sizable slice of corporate America moved large numbers of employees into programs that are far less costly for the corporate bottom line. In 1985, there were approximately 22 million active participants in single-employer defined-benefit plans. Seventeen years later, there were 5 million fewer, despite the fact that the overall U.S. workforce had increased significantly.

Many companies with traditional defined-benefit plans are dumping them onto the Pension Benefit Guaranty Corporation (PBGC). Once used solely as a last resort, shedding retirement obligations is now viewed as just one of many strategic options. Established in 1974 under ERISA following several high-profile benefit program failures, the self-funded PBGC was envisioned as a government-sponsored insurance backstop to protect workers. Like many such programs, however, it had inherent structural flaws and unintended consequences. For one thing, the existence of the PBGC contributed to what is known as "moral hazard." Many companies offered retirement benefits that were overly generous and unsustainable in the long run, knowing full well that if the burden eventually became too great, they could walk away from their obligations.

The fees that the Pension Benefit Guaranty Corporation charged also turned out to be too low, given the risks involved. Following several large corporate failures, including United Airlines, which swamped the agency with liabilities, PBGC found itself

$23 billion in the red at the end of 2005. By some estimates, that amount could exceed $100 billion over 20 years in the absence of dramatic changes. Even that figure may be optimistic. At the end of 2004, the PBGC calculated that America's single-company defined-benefit plans were underfunded by as much as $450 billion, with nearly $300 billion of that total not reflected on company balance sheets, compared to a deficit of $164 billion only three years earlier.

Although the PBGC is not explicitly backed by the government, the federally sponsored agency's insolvency would not necessarily eliminate the problem. Most observers expect that the pension insurer would have to be bailed out despite the political fallout.

Private-pension accounting also has a number of shortcomings, and it has become increasingly obvious that many companies offering such plans have been gaming the system for years. They either assumed that they would earn higher rates of return on their portfolios than was reasonable or underestimated the effects of inflation. Incredibly, some companies borrowed money when interest rates were near their lows after the stock market bubble burst and managed to convert the financing into an instant arbitrage profit. How? They assumed they would earn more on their investments than the interest they would have to pay out on the loans. Under the regulations, they could immediately book the difference as income.

Pension accounting rules also allowed companies to "smooth" returns to avoid creating excessive volatility in reported results. While the allowance had practical value, the methodology tended to obscure the poor state of many plans, especially following the collapse in share prices after March 2000.

This was one reason why the Financial Accounting Standards Board (FASB) stepped in. Similar in scope to the role of its sister agency, GASB, in setting state and local government accounting protocols, FASB decided to rework the rules to provide more insight into corporate America's financial condition. The effort would be a two-stage process. The first step, effective December 15, 2006, requires companies to shift details on the net exposure of pension and other postemployment benefit programs from the footnotes to the balance sheet, directly impacting reported net worth, or assets minus liabilities.

Although in theory there will be no new revelations, the FASB rules will make the data more readily accessible. The hope is to cast a brighter light on poor planning and potential trouble spots. However, the sudden realization that many leading companies are in a precarious financial condition—which, again, should not be a surprise—will likely add to the pressures felt everywhere else. Investors will realize—belatedly—that numerous leading blue-chip companies are more or less insolvent.

The second of the proposed changes in pension accounting rules will be more wide ranging and controversial. Once fully in place, the rule will bring a measure of consistency to the many assumptions that companies make about their pension plans and will likely phase out the smoothing of portfolio returns.

Taken together, all of the new rules will almost certainly have severe repercussions for the bottom line of many companies.

The accounting overseers aren't the only ones making adjustments. In the summer of 2006, Congress and the Bush administration passed a 907-page pension reform bill spurred in part by the widely publicized losses at the PBGC and growing pressure for more accountability. But rather than strengthening the system, many observers believe the measure will do the opposite. Whether the changes will still allow too many loopholes for pension chicanery or spur companies into watering down or eliminating retirement programs, the eventual fallout will only add to the strain on the pension guaranty system and leave more Americans at risk during their twilight years.

For the defined-benefit plans that remain in force, some proposed changes may trigger collateral damage. Budgeting pressures may inspire some pension managers to adjust the mix of assets in their portfolios to reduce swings in net exposure. According to the Committee on Investment of Employee Benefit Assets, the wholesale switch from a smoothing of returns to "mark-to-market" methods, where portfolios are valued based on current prices, could cause $290 billion to be shifted from stocks to bonds, triggering shock waves in both markets. In addition, growing cost pressures will no doubt force many companies to further pare health care and other benefits for retirees and current workers. Increasing numbers will also rely on "financial engineering" strategies or the bankruptcy courts to transfer their existing burdens onto the PBGC or employees.

While some companies will improve their outlook, the overall picture will likely grow worse. Although individuals will have a greater say in their retirement, they will, in reality, have less control over their destiny. One reason is that few people will have much to work with. According to a May 2005 report in the *Washington Post*, "The median account balance of 401(k) and individual retirement accounts combined . . . for households headed by individuals on the verge of retirement [was] $10,000." That is—and will be—a far cry from what they would need to live on without other income, such as from a traditional defined-benefit pension, to supplement it.

Many Americans will likely struggle to keep working well beyond the traditional retirement age, or they will try to turn to an overstretched or already failed social safety net for help. Some may have nowhere to go. Meanwhile, faced with a broad array of pressing financial concerns, state and local governments, as well as the federal government will also look to dump some of their no-longer-tenable promises. In the spring of 2006, the *Wall Street Journal* noted that many states had implemented rules requiring health insurers to cover the adult children of members still living at home. Massachusetts, meanwhile, planned to introduce statewide health insurance funded by a mandatory fee on employers and individuals.

But in the end, such measures won't bridge the gap. They will merely shift a portion of the burden to a different spot, like the air in a squeezed balloon. As the pressures from an unwinding debt bubble, a falling housing market, and a collapsing economy continue to grow, the retirement system and other wobbly towers of promises-to-be-broken will soon come tumbling down.

GOVERNMENT GUARANTEES

"The only sure thing about luck is that it will change."
—Bret Harte

In 1968, Vermont enacted a ban on billboards and roadside advertising to protect its scenic views. According to the *Concise Encyclopedia of Economics,* one consequence "was the appearance of large, bizarre 'sculptures' adjacent to businesses." These included a 12-foot tall, 16-ton gorilla clutching a real Volkswagen Beetle placed next to a car dealer, and a 19-foot genie holding a rolled carpet as he emerged from a smoking teapot, which was erected near a store that sold floor coverings.

Not exactly what lawmakers had intended when they had passed the measure.

Government efforts at constructing a financial safety net to protect Americans—covering an estimated $6 trillion in claims, according to the Center on Federal Financial Institutions—have led to similarly unexpected, though more pernicious, outcomes. Take the Federal Deposit Insurance Corporation (FDIC), for example. Set up in 1934 by the U.S. government in response to the large number of bank failures during the Great Depression, the FDIC was designed to ensure that small depositors in particular would not be wiped out if a lender shut its doors.

Although the FDIC was structured as an insurance program, with fees levied on participating financial institutions to cover the risk of loss, the ultimate responsibility for making good on depositors' accounts rested with the federal government. And for a long time, the system seemed to work, with less instability and fewer bank runs than had once been common. But eventually the so-called benefit will turn out to have been seriously destabilizing because of the "moral hazard" problem.

Because of the FDIC, those who are covered—customers with deposits of up to $100,000, in most cases—have less incentive to be as vigilant about their own interests as they would without such a backstop. In fact, this paradox is associated with any type of insurance protection. In contrast, prior to 1934, depositors who were worried about getting their money back would quickly move funds to another financial institution at the first sign of trouble.

Moreover, research and anecdotal evidence suggest that cheap, relatively immobile deposits have a perverse effect on lending institutions. Aware that problematic behavior is unlikely to trigger a rush for the exits, banks have an incentive to take on large amounts of risk. And over time, many have. Eventually, intense competition and pressure for deregulation only worsen the moral hazard effect. Like drivers with free or low-cost insurance coverage who are not penalized for accidents, bankers seemingly have little choice but to operate ever more recklessly, especially when their competitors are doing the same.

Compounding the problem is the nature of the system itself. In the United States, lending institutions operate using a fractional reserve-based lending model. Typically, the Federal Reserve sets a minimum level of funds that must be held in case depositors come calling. Banks can then lend out or invest the rest pretty much as they please. In effect, if a financial institution has $1 million in "demand deposits" (e.g., checking accounts), and the required reserve ratio is 10 percent, fractional reserve banking can turn that sum into $10 million worth of loans, as will be shown later. This allows the bank to operate with tremendous leverage, which has risks of its own, of course. Aside from that, banking is like any other business. Managers entrusted to generate high returns are increasingly drawn to opportunities that appear to offer the best rewards—and, very often, the greatest risk.

Alas, when the 1980s rolled around, one group of financial institutions became the poster children for the unintended consequences of federal deposit insurance. The savings and loans, or S&Ls, had long toiled in the sleepy backwaters of traditional mortgage lending. That is, until they were set free to compete with banks and other financial operators. By the time it was all over, a combination of poor management, ill-conceived forays into unfamiliar and risky investments, naiveté, fraud, and a cornucopia of regulatory blunders cost more than $150 billion—approximately $240 billion in 2006 dollars—in a taxpayer-funded bailout.

After the debacle, Washington felt a great deal of pressure to minimize the open-ended nature of the government backstop, and in 1991, the Federal Deposit Insurance Corporation Improvement Act, or FDICIA, was voted into law. This statute mandated that the capital of FDIC-insured institutions would form the primary line of defense once the designated reserve ratio (DRR)—the required proportion of reserves to insured deposits—had been breached as a result of failure-related losses. If that happened, most FDIC-insured banks would be hit with predetermined assessments, based on the amount of their insured deposits and various measures that gauged how prudently they were managed. The charges would continue until the DRR was replenished to the mandated target rate of 1.25 percent of insured deposits.

The FDICIA also scaled back the too-big-to-fail rule, or TBTF. That tenet was based on the longstanding, widely held belief that, while it would be bad policy for the government to bail out all failed institutions—because of the moral hazard implications— there could be a "systemic risk" if a large financial operator was allowed to go under. In other words, the collapse of a major player could trigger a chain reaction that forced other, smaller banks into insolvency and inspire a contagious loss of confidence. Such a collapse might also endanger critical components of the economy's banking system and financial underpinnings, such as payment and securities settlement mechanisms.

Under the new arrangements, if an FDIC-insured institution considered TBTF was faced with insolvency, the government would provide interim support but only after multiple parties, including the Federal Reserve, had agreed to the designation. Ultimately, other large banks, not their smaller brethren, would be responsible for paying the cost of such bailouts. The idea was that no one would be enthusiastic about pulling the plug on a large rival unless it was absolutely, positively necessary.

Yet in spite of the reforms—or because of them—federal deposit insurance continued to create unintended consequences. For one thing, the existence of the financial safety net played an ongoing role in encouraging banks to take on more and more risk—as did a 35 percent rise in insured deposits from 1999 through 2005. This increase was aided by innovations such as the Certificate of Deposit Account Registry Service, or CDARS, a product that allows depositors with larger amounts to skirt FDIC ceilings easily by seamlessly tapping a network of banks around the country.

Banks were growing flush with low-cost "loans"—deposits— from people who were relatively relaxed about how the money was used. Competition from a variety of other operators, including securities firms, foreign banking groups, and corporate America, also meant that traditional lending institutions were constantly striving to reduce low-earning capital cushions or otherwise maximize their returns, often at the expense of traditional prudence.

Some activities were geared toward fee generation, such as the securitization of mortgages, credit card receivables, or other assets, or they catered to low-income individuals with limited options who could be nickeled and dimed to death with charges, including monthly maintenance, ATM fees, and a panoply of other service-related fees. Others revolved around risks off the balance sheet. Some key measures of capital adequacy were typically unaffected by such transactions, regardless of the volumes involved.

These transactions included a vast array of increasingly exotic derivatives and services such as "loan commitments," for which a bank would receive payment up front in exchange for providing future funding. Many institutions also became heavily involved in financing the riskiest kinds of borrowers, including those characterized as subprime and those speculating in real estate. Construction and development lending, for example, rose 33 percent in 2005 to the highest rate since 1986, according to *Slate*.

At the same time, technology, innovation, and a widespread push to realize economy-of-scale efficiencies spurred never-ending consolidation in the financial services industry. Aided by the passage of the Gramm-Leach-Bliley Act of 1999, which allowed banks, securities firms, and insurance companies to join together under one holding company umbrella, the big were getting bigger.

Growing as large as possible made sense, considering how the too-big-too-fail doctrine had been restructured under FDICIA. More than likely, those that were unequivocally classified as TBTF would be bailed out if circumstances took an ugly turn. Most people assumed that Washington would find it politically unpalatable to allow one of the nation's largest financial institutions to go under. As a result, the ten largest banks in the United States controlled 44 percent of industry assets in 2005 versus 17 percent in 1990. Ironically, this development more or less ensured that the failure of one large operator would erupt into the sort of systemic spasm that policymakers had long feared.

Making matters more precarious is that a long overdue economic slowdown or turn in the credit cycle will almost certainly decimate the financial position of America's biggest banks. The risks stem from outsized exposure to property lending and real estate–related activities, financing and trading with highly leveraged hedge funds, and providing credit facilities to shaky companies that will exercise the unwelcome right to borrow money when they cannot get it from anywhere else.

Indeed, by virtue of competitive forces, national regulatory standards, and risk management systems, odds are that most large lenders will likely be in the same leaky boat. Under the circumstances, the failure of even one will quickly deplete the $50 billion in reserves that serve as the backstop for around $4 trillion in insured deposits. Other institutions, especially large peers who will invariably face troubles of their own, will then be in the position of having to siphon off precious capital to others when they need it most for themselves.

This possibility may have motivated 2006 legislation that gave the FDIC discretion to let the designated reserve ratio fluctuate in a wider band. It also permitted "smoothing," whereby reserves could be replenished with assessments spread over five years. But rather than improving matters during a financial downturn, this provision will allow large losses that might once have been dealt with quickly to fester until the problem worsens dramatically, ultimately forcing taxpayers to get involved.

More worrisome is that the same influences have been at play in the securitized mortgage financing market, though the risks could be far more significant. Fannie Mae and Freddie Mac are government-sponsored enterprises that were created by federal charter and instilled with the mission of helping to make mortgages more readily available. Although their debts are not explicitly guaranteed by the government, investors and bankers have long assumed that Washington would be forced to step in should disaster strike.

Along with similar entities like the Federal Home Loan Banks, both GSEs served their purpose by borrowing at relatively cheap rates in the wholesale markets and using the funds to purchase mortgages from lending institutions, thus expanding overall capacity. But it was only a matter of time until the combination of moral hazard, unintended consequences of government actions, and an increasingly competitive financial services environment transformed their mission into a crisis.

Arguably, the turning point for both agencies occurred when they were converted into public companies. Once known as the less sexy-sounding Federal National Mortgage Association, Fannie

Mae was privatized in 1970. Originally part of the Federal Home Loan Bank system, sister agency Freddie Mac was privatized in 1989. Like the S&Ls during the 1980s, Fannie and Freddie were suddenly free of regulatory burdens and forced to compete with more experienced, sophisticated, and aggressive financial firms in a rapidly changing marketplace.

In large part, they capitalized on their inherent advantages: their established position at the center of the mortgage universe and the widespread perception that their bonds and other obligations were nearly as good as government-issued debt. Fannie and Freddie became master securitizers, buying up tremendous numbers of mortgages from a wide range of loan "originators"— banks, thrifts, and specialized mortgage finance companies—and repackaging them into mortgage-backed (MBSs)securities with a guarantee slapped on for good measure. Then they sold these MBSs to large and small fixed-income investors, state and local governments, foreign central banks, and a wide range of other banks and financial services firms.

The securitization process proved to be a virtual circle, generating fees for everyone involved, serving as a wellspring of almost unlimited credit that supplanted traditional financing sources, and helping to raise the American home ownership rate from around 64 percent in 1990 to a record 69.2 percent 14 years later.

Yet along with ultralow interest rates and the active participation of the financial services industry, Fannie and Freddie also helped to boost total mortgage debt to nearly $9 trillion—approximately three-quarters of the GDP and an increase of 42 percent from the levels seen during the 2001 recession. By 2005, the two agencies were guarantors on more than $2 trillion of mortgage-backed securities.

The competitive pressures of the marketplace demanded more. Over time, Fannie Mae and Freddie Mac also became two of the world's largest speculators. And without the restraint of market discipline—counterparties pulling the plug out of fear that their activities might be too risky—there was little to stop them. Relying on their capacity to borrow almost limitless sums of money at rates only marginally higher than those the federal government paid, they built highly leveraged portfolios of MBSs of nearly $1.5 trillion—many of which they had issued themselves—and other debt obligations. Legally, the GSEs were only required to back the assets with capital of 2.5 percent. For the mortgage-backed securities they guaranteed, the ratio was less than one-half percent. This exposed Fannie and Freddie to enormous interest rate, credit, and repayment risk. The latter danger reflects that borrowers can pay off the underlying loan at any time, and if a number of borrowers whose debts collateralize the MBS make the same decision, their collective actions can shorten or lengthen the effective maturity date—and hence the value—of the security, creating costly pricing uncertainty.

But it seemed that Fannie Mae and Freddie Mac were not just going to roll the dice. They decided that the key to managing risk was to actively buy and sell securities. They also made use of the rapidly expanding market for interest rate and other complex derivatives, which are, at their core, leveraged bets on a particular event or outcome. Instead of being exposed solely to honoring a guarantee on some proportion of the securities they backed, Fannie and Freddie would have to deal with many other potential uncertainties. And they had to do so successfully if the banks, which owned a combined $1 trillion of direct debt and MBSs issued by the two behemoths, were to avoid paying a devastating price.

In almost no time at all, the two GSEs had joined the ranks of the too-big-to-fail crowd.

Still, Washington and the financial community gave them the benefit of the doubt, as both were frequent beneficiaries of the GSEs' largesse. So did the Office of Federal Housing Enterprise Oversight, which seemed more of a cheerleader than a regulatory overseer, until investigations in 2003 and 2004 revealed a host of accounting irregularities at the two mortgage giants. Both had "smoothed" results to meet internal performance-related criteria and keep Wall Street happy.

The investigations forced the two institutions to delay earnings reports and issue restatements. In November 2005, Fannie Mae disclosed $10.8 billion in accounting errors stemming from its derivatives and hedging activities and noted that it didn't expect to complete its 2004 annual report before the second half of 2006. Despite hearings, investigations, and resignations, as well as repeated calls for their portfolios to be downsized and their capital requirements to be raised, Fannie and Freddie remain active players in both the mortgage and derivatives markets. In many respects, the situation is not unlike what happened in the 1980s, when inaction and delay—what some refer to as "regulatory forbearance"—ultimately contributed to the much higher than expected $150 billion cost of the S&L crisis.

But there is more to the budding crisis in the financial safety net than pension guarantees, deposit insurance, and government-sponsored enterprises. The federal government has become increasingly exposed to other, less-quantifiable risks. One of these dangers is the direct and indirect cost of natural and human-made catastrophes.

In 2005, Hurricane Katrina wiped out much of New Orleans and tore through wide swaths of the Gulf Coast region. Following broad political pressure and a wave of recriminations, the federal government ponied up more than $100 billion, a figure expected to rise. Other disasters, including the September 11 terrorist attacks, also triggered an ad hoc response, with Washington authorizing at least $20 billion for New York alone. That event also led to the creation of the Terrorism Risk Insurance Act of 2002, which provided a backstop of $100 billion a year in the event of similar hostilities.

These developments lend further credence to the dangerous assumption that the federal government will pick up the tab for virtually any disaster, including the failure of a large financial institution or one of the many guaranty funds and insurers of last resort, or ILRs, around the country.

Some ILRs are state backed, while others are not. Set up in most cases to cover risks that the private sector would not—or could not—underwrite, many have been faced with growing financial problems exacerbated by political meddling, poor management, and artificially low premiums. For example, following the strong hurricane season in 2005, Florida's state-sponsored insurer, Citizens Property Insurance Corporation, was in the hole for $1.7 billion, more than triple 2004's total. This prompted widespread calls for a taxpayer bailout. According to the *Wall Street Journal,* more than half of all such ILRs had deficits as of 2003, the last year for which data were available.

Because nonbank financial institutions play a largely hidden but otherwise substantial role in the financial system, they also represent a sizable risk for markets and for the federal government. These include the four AAA-rated—as of 2006—private insurers that back 80 percent of the $2 trillion municipal bond market, often with capital cushions of less than 2 percent. One firm, MBIA, guarantees nearly $900 billion of state and local government obligations. With municipal and corporate credit ratings under pressure and bankruptcies on the rise, one or more of the guarantors will almost certainly find their perceived financial strength being called into question, a development that will trigger shock waves across the fixed-income markets.

But whether or not the government mops up these budding disasters, the political, financial, and social fallout as the unraveling gets under way will be devastating and widespread. There are too many links in the chain and too many points of vulnerability in the financial system, especially for commercial banks, which have been some of the most aggressive contributors to the recent credit bubble expansion. Ironically, a 2006 report that the FDIC was disbanding many bank closure teams because of a lack of failures may well have been one of the most ironic moments in the long and sorry saga of moral hazard and unintended consequences. Like dominos, when one begins to fall, the others won't soon be far behind.

4

DERIVATIVES

"Beware of silent dogs and still water."
—Latin proverb

Warren Buffett, chair of Berkshire Hathaway, has long warned about the dangers of derivatives. With firsthand experience unraveling thousands of complex transactions at Berkshire-owned General Re at a cost of over $400 million, he undoubtedly knows what he's talking about. He also has a history of writing about matters that concern him. So it wasn't all that surprising when he offered up some of his characteristic homespun wisdom on derivatives in the company's 2005 annual report.

Buffett wrote:

> Long ago, Mark Twain said: "A man who tries to carry a cat home by its tail will learn a lesson that can be learned in no other way." If Twain were around now, he might try winding up a derivatives business. After a few days, he would opt for cats.

While the legendary investor's criticisms didn't seem especially out of place, the same cannot be said about comments from other influential experts in recent years.

Timothy Geithner, president of the Federal Reserve Bank of New York, has been uncharacteristically outspoken for a central banker. In a February 2006 speech on dramatic changes in the U.S. and global financial systems during the past quarter century, he began with the typically benign observation that derivatives appeared to have made the financial system "able to absorb more easily a broader array of shocks." But then he added:

> They have not eliminated risk. They have not ended the tendency of markets to [undergo] occasional periods of mania and panic. They have not eliminated the possibility of failure of a major financial intermediary. And they cannot fully insulate the broader financial system from the effects of such a failure.

Mr. Geithner has raised concerns in a number of speeches about operational deficiencies that were undermining the rapidly growing credit derivatives market. He also arranged a series of meetings with senior executives at leading financial institutions to address an alarming backlog of unsettled trades.

Comments from officials like Emil Henry, the U.S. assistant treasury secretary for financial institutions, and Randal K. Quarles, undersecretary for domestic finance, have also been curious, especially in respect to hedge fund managers, the relatively new kids in the investment world. At an April 2006 conference, Mr. Henry expressed concerns about the systemic risks posed by the "nexus of hedge funds and the OTC [over-the-counter] derivatives market, especially credit derivatives," and suggested that the "Treasury should get its arms around this." A month earlier, Mr. Quarles stated that, "[a] smaller number of larger firms, both banks and nonbanks, have assumed systemic importance." He noted: "The rapid growth of the housing GSEs . . . and the increased demand for their securities . . . have greatly exacerbated the potential for events at these institutions to have systemic consequences."

The International Monetary Fund (IMF) also wasn't uttering bureaucratic happy-talk in its 2006 "Global Financial Stability Report" when it raised the prospect of "liquidity disturbances" in the derivatives market. In fact, the IMF seemed downright pessimistic when it suggested, according to Reuters, that "[i]nvestors in structured credit products risk not being able to sell or obtain an acceptable price following a market downturn because buyers may shun the fast-growing market."

The decision in 2005 to reconvene the Counterparty Risk Management Group—first formed in 1999 after the meltdown of hedge fund Long-Term Capital Management—to explore risks in the American financial system was hardly routine. Chaired by E. Gerald Corrigan, Goldman Sachs managing director and former New York Fed president, the group of high-powered movers and shakers highlighted several areas of concern in its 273-page report, including the valuation and pricing of illiquid derivatives, unsettled trades, and other potential systemic risks.

In all of these instances, those in the know appeared to act somewhat atypically. They did not adhere to the longstanding tradition of working behind the scenes to avoid triggering a potential crisis. Even more interesting, they changed their behavior when optimism was high, stock and bond market volatility was low, large financial hiccups had all but disappeared, and economic conditions were widely perceived to be in a Goldilocks state—not too hot, not too cold, but just right. Nonetheless, as with silent dogs—or cats, perhaps—something clearly was amiss.

Their uncharacteristic openness likely reflected mounting concerns that two developments—the growth of the hedge fund industry and the rapidly expanding use of complex derivatives—exerted an increasingly destabilizing influence on the financial system.

Despite its mystique, the original premise behind hedge fund investing is not difficult to understand. In addition to buying stocks that are cheap, money managers could "hedge" those positions by going "short"—placing a negative bet on—shares they deemed overvalued. This strategy, often referred to as market-neutral investing, could in theory generate profits on both sides of the equation as well as lessen exposure to the vagaries of the overall market. For a variety of legal and tax-related reasons, those who practiced this style of investing, especially when the industry was in its infancy, tended to market their expertise to institutions and wealthy individuals. As a result, hedge funds have been lightly regulated.

What really sets hedge funds apart from traditional financial vehicles, however, is that most have been structured around a performance-based compensation system. Rather than being paid solely on the basis of assets under management, like mutual fund managers, hedge fund advisors are paid an incentive fee based on how well they do. In other words, relative performance—making more than the next guy—matters less than absolute returns—making money in good times and bad.

In general, hedge fund advisors get a cut—often around 20 percent—of annual returns above a preset benchmark, or "hurdle" rate. This is in addition to a fee, typically 2 percent, of the total funds under management. As it happens, the profit-sharing aspect, without an offsetting downside when performance suffers, is a powerful catalyst to get involved in activities with the greatest upside potential—but often the biggest downside risk. Hedge funds are frequently lean organizations, free of many traditional operating and regulatory constraints, so their managers tend to be more active, opportunistic, and freewheeling than "long-only" fiduciaries. Over time, the pursuit of profitable opportunities has led hedge fund advisors to move away from the original "long-short equity" concept. They have branched out into a variety of other products and markets and adopted increasingly sophisticated strategies for making money. Many have also grown comfortable using large dollops of debt to boost returns.

Hedge funds represented just a fraction of the overall investing universe in the decades after the first one appeared in 1949. Until the mid-1990s, in fact, few outside Wall Street had been aware of their existence, except for occasional stories about very successful operators such as George Soros. But after the stock market bubble burst in the spring of 2000, all that changed. Suddenly nervous investors began to look for "alternative" arrangements that could help them weather—and hopefully profit from—similarly unsettling conditions in the future.

At the same time, a poor operating environment and falling revenues spurred investment banks and brokerage firms to focus their attentions on this increasingly active, rapidly expanding group. But the banks and brokerages weren't just executing their transactions and financing their positions; many on Wall Street switched sides to become "hedgies" themselves. This shift helped spur a more aggressive and rapid-fire approach to making money throughout the consolidating financial services industry. Not surprisingly, the generous compensation structure, heightened competition, and widespread emphasis on absolute performance have had a powerful influence on behavior.

The focus in the hedge fund community, and around much of Wall Street, has increasingly been to generate the highest possible returns in the shortest amount of time. This perspective dovetails nicely with a more generalized move toward greater risk taking that federal deposit insurance promulgated. It wasn't exactly a recipe for patience, prudent stewardship, and anticipatory thinking about long-term consequences. More likely, it was the reason why hedge funds, banks, insurers, and many other members of the global financial services community boosted their involvement in the derivatives market.

When people hear the word *derivatives*, their eyes tend to glaze over. Most outside the world of finance view the term as a largely irrelevant and intangible construct of academics and Wall Street rocket scientists. But derivative securities have become an integral part of the financial world, and numerous innovations that people take for granted, such as low-priced and flexible mortgage financing, depend on the use of these synthetically created instruments.

Unfortunately, they have also turned out to be, to use an old expression, the "tail wagging the dog" in many equity, fixed-income, and commodity markets, a situation that has created significant risks for Wall Street and Main Street.

Simply put, a derivative is a financial instrument whose value depends on, or is derived from, something else, such as a stock, a bond, a loan, a commodity, the weather, or an event. One example is an equity option whereby an investor pays a premium for the right to buy or sell a share at a fixed price on or before a certain date. Another is a mortgage-backed security made up of loans from many different borrowers pooled together and sold as a package or series of customized tranches. In this case, the value of the MBS ultimately depends on the money flowing into and out of a specially created shell company, or SPV, and the behavior of the underlying borrowers. Most of the well-known basket-type products, such as stock index futures and exchange-traded funds, or ETFs, are also derivatives. Typically, they represent an interest in a bundle of shares or other assets, but they have no intrinsic worth of their own. If the value of what is in the bundle increases, so does the price of the ETF.

But there are many other varieties of derivatives, some involving factors and contingencies that are not as readily explained. The pricing of options, for example, is influenced by the time remaining until maturity, interest rates, and investor expectations about how volatile markets will be. Some varieties include complicated derivatives that depend on other derivatives for their value. Most of the synthetically created securities that many firms hold in sizable portfolios cannot be understood, let alone managed, without relying on complicated formulas and powerful computers.

Derivatives tend to fall into two categories: exchange traded or over the counter (OTC). Listed contracts like S&P 500 futures normally have standardized terms and trade at established venues such as the Chicago Board of Trade. Typically, a central clearinghouse acts as the settlement counterparty on every deal to ensure that things run smoothly.

In contrast, OTC derivatives are ad hoc arrangements tailored to the needs of those directly involved in each transaction, though industry trade bodies like the International Securities Dealers Association (ISDA) frequently set standards for terminology and settlement practices. Unlike the exchange-traded markets, where regulators closely monitor activity, the over-the-counter market has remained fairly opaque and thus hard to quantify in the aggregate. While partly due to the customization of deals, the opacity is also a direct result of the industry's light regulation.

That derivatives are global by nature, involving institutions from many countries with varying or even minimal regulatory regimes, tends to reinforce their obscurity. Cynically, or perhaps realistically, one can assume that the lack of transparency has also suited those who have been active in these instruments. Commercial and investment banks have capitalized on widespread ignorance of the inner workings of complex derivatives, especially with regard to the risks involved, the purpose of the more exotic creations, and the profit margins that they make. According to TowerGroup, U.S. brokerage firms were expected to generate $33.2 billion from derivatives-related revenue in 2006.

Many kinds of derivatives also have certain structural features that make them appealing to hedge funds, speculators, and others. All it takes to create one of these instruments is an agreement between two counterparties. When they involve a future promise, derivatives are frequently treated as off-balance-sheet obligations, which means they are not accounted for in the same way as are other financial instruments. In that case, companies, banks, and brokers often don't have to allocate precious capital to backstop the exposure, even though the risk of loss is still present. In a few respects, this treatment mirrors that of retiree health care benefits, where a prospective and often sizable future cost is not fully reflected on current financial statements.

The upside to treating risk as being off the balance sheet is that capital can be much more efficiently employed, creating, in effect, what could be described as operational leverage, whereby a little bit of money can go a long way. The downside, however, is that these transactions can obscure the potentially dangerous exposure that firms have. They can also be used to circumvent regulatory requirements and to transform, time shift, or hide financial and economic activities, such as capital gains and income, and to avoid taxes.

Such machinations have involved the garden-variety incentive stock options that technology firms and others have increasingly used to offer compensation that is heavily geared to the share price of the company in question. During 2006, a scandal erupted because many publicly listed businesses had backdated outstanding options so they appeared to have been issued when the share price was at its lowest point for the year, or they doled out options to executives just before bullish announcements. Agence France-Presse reported in September 2006 that the U.S. Securities and Exchange Commission (SEC) was "investigating over 100 companies, including some of America's biggest corporations, for possible stock options fraud."

Because these instruments are constructed virtually out of thin air, no money needs to change hands at the outset (as is the case with listed contracts) unless required under the terms of the agreement or by the nature of the marketplace in which they trade. In the oil futures market, for example, two sides can agree to strike a deal based on the current price that allows the buyer to deliver a set quantity and quality of the commodity to the seller before a predetermined date. According to New York Mercantile Exchange rules, both are required to put up a "good faith" deposit, known as a "margin," to ensure that they honor their commitments.

But when a relatively small amount of such collateral is involved—or in the case of an option contract, where premium payments are typically a fraction of the face, or "notional," value of the deal—that represents a form of leverage. For a small down payment, one can control an asset worth many times that much. Although not inherent in all derivatives, the prospect of getting more bang for your buck—perhaps a whole lot more—through leverage has considerable appeal to those trying to make the most of their capital, especially if, like hedge fund managers, they stand to benefit directly from good performance.

To be sure, derivatives have considerable value when used as a hedge to shift or rearrange risks. In one type of contract called a "swap," two counterparties agree to exchange payments over a set period, allowing each to alter their exposure to market forces or to benefit from any comparative advantages they might have. Banks, for instance, have often used interest rate swaps. In a hypothetical example, they might agree to make fixed payments over five years in exchange for receiving floating-rate payments that might normally fluctuate over time. This enables the institutions to better match the cash flows of the loans they have granted and the bonds they own to the payments they must make to depositors and other creditors, thus reducing the risk of loss if market rates move the "wrong" way.

But in recent years, another type of swap transaction has risen to prominence, one that is causing growing concern among regulators. Known as credit default swaps, or CDSs, they make up the fastest-growing segment of the $370 global derivatives market.

Simply put, a CDS is a bet on a company's financial health that allows counterparties to take on or shed credit risk. In a typical example, the side assuming the risk sells protection covering the value of a bond or other obligation in case a default, bankruptcy, or other "credit event" occurs. In exchange, the buyer of what is essentially a form of insurance pays an annual fee over the life of the agreement and, in some cases, another amount up front, with the total depending on the degree of perceived risk of the underlying borrower. Should one of the prescribed events take place, the buyer would deliver the covered bond or other obligation, which is likely to be worth much less than its face value because of the company's financial troubles. The protection seller, in turn, hands over the amount they originally agreed upon.

Traded over the counter, these agreements are generally struck without the knowledge of anyone besides the two counterparties—

not even the company whose fortunes are being wagered on. This creates the potential for excessively large—and destabilizing—derivatives exposure relative to the risks being covered, leaving open the possibility that a single credit-related development could have far-reaching consequences.

For example, when auto parts maker Delphi filed for bankruptcy protection in October 2005, reports indicated more than $20 billion in credit default contracts had been written on $2 billion of outstanding bonds. By the spring of 2006, at least $200 billion of General Motors's CDSs were estimated to exist, covering $30 billion of bonds. Aside from the tail wagging and other market distortions, as well as the upheaval such a mismatch can cause, there is also the very real risk that major financial operators could find themselves in over their heads, leading to dangerous systemic pressures.

Still, these instruments suit a wide range of interests. Many banks, for instance, have been keen to reshuffle risks to free up capital for other uses, whereas insurers and hedge funds have relished the opportunity to offer the promise of protection—often with little or no collateral involved—for what seems like easy money. Not surprisingly, interest in credit default swaps has spread like wildfire. By the second quarter of 2006, the notional value of outstanding CDSs had grown to $26 trillion, a 109 percent gain from a year earlier and a far cry from less than $1 trillion in 2001.

Some argue that any discussion of notional values tends to exaggerate the risks involved. Using the earlier example of an interest rate swap, for instance, if a deal was struck that made reference to an underlying value of $1 million, it would not necessarily mean that one counterparty would stand to lose that much if the other side defaulted. In this case, the amount of potential loss would tend to be linked to the difference between the fixed-rate and floating-rate interest payments, which would be significantly smaller than the reported value. The notional amount of principal in such transactions—in this case, $1 million—wouldn't actually change hands, meaning the exposure is less than it seems.

However, with other types of derivatives, including credit default swaps, the amount at risk could be significant if the counterparty who sold the protection either walks away from the deal or goes bust. The risk could even be as much as the entire face amount. For instance, regulators have realized that in the absence of a written confirmation, some counterparties will almost certainly deny that a transaction took place if the "covered" company goes belly up. That is why Mr. Geithner and others raised the alarm when reports surfaced in 2005 that more than 100,000 CDSs had been verbally agreed to but not settled. Even though those efforts helped reduce the backlog, thousands of transactions still remained in a state of limbo as of mid-2006.

Already disputes and lawsuits have arisen over existing CDSs and other derivative agreements stemming from ambiguous terminology, valuation discrepancies, and the fact that certain corporate developments, such as restructurings, were not anticipated when deals were struck. Evidence that many transactions have been "assigned," or transferred, to another party by one of the original sides to the deal without the knowledge of the initial counterparty has only made matters worse, though new rules adopted during 2006 were designed to mitigate that risk.

Even so, despite recent efforts to address at least some of the concerns, past and present structural deficiencies have laid the groundwork for a chaotic and possibly nightmarish scenario. Those who believed they were covered might be left scrambling to hedge their sudden and unexpected exposure, desperate to make up the shortfall under conditions of duress.

But the systemic risks do not only stem from a particular instrument or market. They exist also because of the concentration of exposure at certain large commercial banking groups, including JPMorgan Chase, Bank of America, Citibank, Wachovia, and HSBC. According to data collected by the U.S. Comptroller of the Currency, as of the fourth quarter of 2005, these five institutions accounted for 96 percent of the more than $100 trillion of derivatives contracts outstanding among 836 U.S. banks. Remember, too, the exposure of Fannie Mae and Freddie Mac, who have $1.5 trillion of derivatives between them to hedge against risks in their massive portfolios.

Many regulators and people in the industry itself argue that the decidedly lopsided concentration of derivatives is not as bad as it looks. The largest commercial banking groups typically have the most sophisticated risk management systems and access to resources and counterparties that might not be available to smaller peers. Soothsayers also contend that the gross notional exposure exaggerates the risks, because a significant volume of transactions are interest rate swaps, for example.

So-called netting agreements minimize the dangers even further. Under such agreements, when banks have multiple contracts outstanding with the same counterparty, they agree to tally the total value of what they owe versus what they are due, calculated in present value terms, to arrive at a net exposure, which is typically far smaller than the gross amount. Even on this basis, the overall derivatives-related net credit risk exceeded $1 trillion in the commercial banking sector at the end of 2005.

But that doesn't include unforeseen circumstances that might lead to differences of opinion, liquidity issues, or torrents of litigation about the value of individual agreements. Nor does it consider the possibility that if one bank gets into trouble, others will be less than cooperative as they face major problems of their own. And even if the banks come to an arrangement among themselves, it will not necessarily address the potential fallout from their exposure to counterparties such as the GSEs, hedge funds, securities firms, and finance arms of large multinational corporations. Hedge funds, for example, accounted for 55 percent of credit derivatives trading in the year through March 2006, according to Greenwich Associates.

Although these concerns will only become more critical when the economic situation takes a turn for the worse, the real dangers are likely to stem from seriously flawed assumptions and conflicts of interest. Despite the involvement of Wall Street's best and brightest—academics, rocket scientists, and programmers—and the sense of mathematical certitude conveyed through the use of complex calculations and high-powered computers, pricing derivatives involves a significant amount of guesswork that is not necessarily unbiased. Often, expectations are drawn from historical patterns that, for many newfangled varieties, are woefully incomplete. Or they are based on how other securities are trading, without taking into account differences that gain importance under stressful market conditions.

Other problems are likely to arise following sizable issuance in recent years of so-called hybrid securities, which act like bonds under certain circumstances and stocks at other times. In 2006, the National Association of Insurance Commissioners (NAIC) caused shock waves when it ruled that insurance company buyers should treat certain hybrids as equity rather than debt, reducing their appeal because of the additional capital cushion required. Following the uproar, the NAIC backpedaled and announced that it would set up a commission to study the issue instead.

Some incredibly complex securities, formed from multiple layers of derivatives, can exhibit a uniquely dangerous phenomenon known as "cliff risk." Rather than gradually adjusting to a continuing series of negative developments, these toxic monstrosities can go from highly rated obligations to "junk," with their price falling in lockstep after just one additional measure of bad news. A single straw, suddenly and without warning, can break the camel's back.

Of course, it remains to be seen how synthetically created securities and derivative portfolios with multiple influences and unstable statistical relationships will react under uniquely unsettling circumstances. Credit derivatives have never been tested in times of acute market stress, such as a collapse of the real estate market, a cratering economy, or volatile market conditions like the 1987 stock market crash. And beyond what is euphemistically referred to as "model failure," the coming upheaval will almost certainly reveal the nefarious and not-so-nefarious influences that have been allowed to fester because of a destructive incentive compensation structure and a lack of transparency.

These problems include mistakes and back-office snafus, intentional mispricing and fraud, and inappropriate accounting for derivatives exposure. All of these are likely to reveal a sizable gap between reported and actual valuations, which will have a calamitous impact on a wide range of markets—not to mention overall confidence in the financial system. Based on a study by the International Swaps and Derivatives Association, for example, 17 percent of credit derivative trade tickets written in 2005 contained errors, compared to 9 percent a year earlier, whereas "rebooking rates" hit 21 percent, "implying erroneous data was entered into risk-management systems before being corrected," according to Reuters.

But unintentional errors are only a part of it. In September 2005, a London-based trader was reportedly suspended by his employer for allegedly covering up a shortfall of more than $50 million by mismarking positions in exotic derivatives. Whereas some might view this as a case of "one bad apple," the alleged misdeed apparently took place over several months at a large global financial institution with sophisticated risk-monitoring systems.

Another casualty of financial chicanery was Fannie Mae, which was forced to recognize billions in losses attributable to a misapplication of what are known as hedge-accounting rules. Under certain circumstances, a company is not required to report the gyrations in income that arise when derivatives and other securities are marked-to-market if they are being used to protect other positions. According to *CFO* magazine, 57 companies made such restatements in 2005 because of faulty hedge accounting, which suggests that more than a little fudging has been going on.

While not specific to derivatives, other dangers lurk and are likely to show up en masse when the tide turns. Many of the largest Wall Street firms rely on similar risk management systems that involve a concept known as value at risk, or VaR. Generally speaking, this measure attempts to quantify the maximum amount that a firm might expect to lose on any given day based on formulas that take into account the theoretical value of outstanding positions and the volatility of markets. According to the *Investment Dealers Digest*, VaR is "a measurement that is increasingly considered incomplete, overly simplistic, or even misleading."

Still, leaving aside the thorny issue of how accurate VaR models will be when circumstances are less benign, the widespread use of such systems creates a fundamental flaw. When the time comes for large operators to pare down positions to reduce risk, many other institutions likely will try to do the same.

In other words, their collective actions will set in motion a vicious feedback loop where each round of sales—or purchases, in the case of bearish bets—stirs up the market even more, triggering a fresh demand for additional rebalancing, especially from the most leveraged, most involved operators. This scenario in itself will impair the value of at least some of the collateral in question, causing a death spiral that creates the kinds of systemic dangers about which Mr. Buffett and others have repeatedly warned us. By then, everyone will have realized rather abruptly that the key benefit of derivatives, their so-called ability to transform risks and disperse them widely, is a liability that has destabilized the entire financial system.

RISKS

5

ECONOMIC MALAISE

"The most dangerous thing is illusion."
—Ralph Waldo Emerson

At the August 2000 meeting of the Federal Open Market Committee, the policymaking arm of the Federal Reserve, research director David Stockton noted there was little sign of "an appreciable dent in the demand for equipment and software. It just doesn't look like this boom is about to dissipate any time soon." Unfortunately, his assessment turned out to be wide of the mark. In retrospect, the *Wall Street Journal* reported that, "[a] multiyear tech boom peaked at about that time." Yet it wasn't the only occasion when a central bank official got it wrong. The *New York Times* wrote that former Fed chairman Alan Greenspan, "like most economists, failed to see at first that the economy had tipped from sluggish growth into . . . contraction," during the 1990s.

When it comes to misjudging which way the economic winds are blowing, policymakers aren't alone, of course. Tea leaf readers on Wall Street and those who report on them have often been similarly confounded. According to James Stack, a market historian and editor of *Investech Research*, "not one recession in the past 50 years" was predicted in advance by a major poll of economists.

That is the reality of forecasting: just because you know what happened yesterday doesn't mean you know what will happen tomorrow. That is the case even if the data at hand is timely, accurate, and relevant—often not true of statistics gleaned from an economy as large and diverse as the American economy. More confusing still is that lags in reporting, estimates with large margins of error, or varying sensitivities to changes in the underlying fundamentals invariably offer a less-than-consistent picture when a nation is in the throes of a full-fledged boom or bust.

Problems also stem from the inherent behavioral biases that color the views of even the most nonpartisan observers. These include giving greater weight to more recent events and assuming that existing trends will carry on. Then there is the impact of "groupthink," whereby, to avoid being seen as foolish, everyone avoids promoting viewpoints outside the comfort zone of consensus thinking. Motivation is also a powerful influence. Individuals who work in the public sector, especially those who have been voted into office, or who work for brokers and other businesses that stand to benefit from positive sentiment, frequently find themselves—willingly or not—becoming cheerleaders for a bullish view, regardless of whether the data support it.

More than likely, some combination of these factors accounted for the optimism that prevailed nearly six years after the stock market bubble burst in the spring of 2000. This optimism endured despite growing signs of trouble in several key areas, including the housing market, the domestic automobile industry, and the commodities pits, where prices of gold, oil, and copper had all touched multidecade highs in a frenzy reminiscent of the late 1970s.

Until mid-2006, in fact, the U.S. economy was generally viewed as being in a Goldilocks state. Unfortunately, many observers made the classic miscalculation: they assumed that the disparate pluses and minuses added up to some sort of healthy middle. This is a perspective akin to that of an adventurer wading complacently across an unfamiliar river with an "average" depth of 4 feet—and hidden trenches 20 feet deep.

Everywhere you looked, ominous signs belied the upbeat reports and sustainability of the post-2001 recovery. The personal savings rate had fallen below zero to its lowest levels since the 1930s, indicating that Americans were not socking away anything for a rainy day. Even if they wanted to save, the data suggested it would have been a challenge. Between 2001 and 2004, inflation-adjusted average family income fell by 2 percent, lagging far behind the prior 3-year period's 17 percent increase, according to the Federal Reserve's triennial "Survey of Consumer Finances." Family income also trailed a double-digit gain in gross domestic product.

Not only savings suffered. Many of the less fortunate had struggled to stay afloat after share prices collapsed and the economy then slipped into a brief recession. Indeed, by 2006, "record numbers" of lower-income Americans found themselves "in a more precarious position than at any time in recent memory," as one expert noted in the *New York Times*. With consumer spending accounting for around two-thirds of national output, these tensions framed an economy that seemed balanced precariously on edge amid the bursting bubble. In a sense, the United States looked like a once omnipotent giant poised for a nasty takedown when overburdened households retrenched and reliquified.

But things didn't turn out that way when the economy stalled in 2001, because torrents of fresh spending power—in the form of borrowed money—soon became more readily and widely available, almost regardless of Americans' ability to pay it back. In fact, ample evidence suggests that what kept many people afloat after the 1990s boom ended was debt, especially property-related borrowing, which expanded dramatically on the heels of easy money, relaxed standards, intense competition, and a securitization gold rush enabled by fee-hungry bankers and the likes of Fannie Mae and Freddie Mac.

Paradoxically, perhaps, this resurgent allure of borrowed money coincided with an increasingly widespread search for "safer" and supposedly less volatile alternatives to a risky stock market—a market that had soared dramatically higher and slumped hard as the 20th century came to an end.

The economic impact of the credit-driven bubble that developed in the real estate market proved enormous, whether referring to the jobs that it created directly, the spillover from housing-associated purchases, or the broad boost in spending fed by mortgage equity withdrawals. The stimulus from the "wealth effect" lent further support to domestic consumption, as house prices soared more than 50 percent on average from 2001 to 2005, according to data from the Office of Federal Housing Enterprise Oversight. Many re-embraced the mantra of consumerism and the American dream, and the economy began to recover anew.

The tradeoff was that by early 2006, the United States was "more dependent on housing than it [had] been in a half-century," the *Washington Post* reported, with activity in the real estate sector accounting for "nearly three-quarters of the nation's job growth" since the 2001 recession. During that five-year period, consumers had borrowed an estimated $2.5 trillion in equity from their homes and had spent as much as half of it on other goods and services, from vacations and dining out to cars and college tuitions, according to analysts.

But not only lenders disrupted the economy from its normal cyclical course; central bankers, politicians—including President Bush and the Republican-controlled Congress, by way of several first-term tax cuts—and others also acquiesced to the demands of struggling constituencies. By failing to alleviate the excesses that had built up during previous years, and by allowing overextended individuals and shaky businesses to continue borrowing and spending without taking imbalances into account, these public and private sector enablers laid the groundwork for an even more calamitous ending.

By the summer of 2006, signs of the long-overdue move to the downside cropped up. Many highly paid oracles on Wall Street seemed oblivious to evidence that two years of monetary policy tightening by the Federal Reserve was starting to do harm. Some optimists mistakenly viewed continued refinancing activity as a positive for the economy, believing that it would bolster consumer demand, as it had done since 2001. When interest rates trended lower, many homeowners swapped expensive fixed mortgages for lower-rate loans featuring smaller payments, helping to free up extra spending power every month.

Millions also borrowed more than they needed to cover balances outstanding on existing mortgages. They used the excess funds from these "cash-out refis" for a variety of purposes, including spending on necessities and extravagances, paying off higher-rate credit cards and unsecured loans, and investing in other assets. Even so, it didn't seem encouraging in the first quarter of 2006 when Freddie Mac reported that a record 88 percent of borrowers refinancing existing loans took out more than 5 percent of what they owed. Because most of those who would benefit from swapping costly mortgages for cheaper ones had done so when rates were falling, this borrowing activity smacked of desperation.

The most ominous development was the widespread unraveling of the real estate market, which had become an economic lifeline for many Americans. In the blink of an eye, media outlets around the country, which only months earlier had heralded a long-term property boom, suddenly turned cautious and reported all sorts of bad news. In places like Nevada, Colorado, and Florida, once the hottest real estate markets in the country, sentiment turned abruptly sour as vacancies, inventories, mortgage arrears, and foreclosures soared. Stories also circulated about would-be speculators who walked away from hefty down payments because of falling prices.

But not only the epicenters of the boom were trembling; bubble-trouble was evident across the land. RealtyTrac, an online foreclosure data service, reported in the first quarter of 2006 that the number of mortgage loans around the country that had entered some stage of foreclosure had risen 72 percent in 12 months. Moreover, the backlog of unsold new and existing homes had also increased dramatically—hitting multiyear records—and the National Association of Home Builders' Housing Market Index had fallen to a 15-year low in September. The year-on-year median price for an existing home also declined for the first time in over a decade. "For Sale" signs sprouted like weeds. Even some normally Pollyannaish construction industry insiders were beginning to ponder out loud about a "hard landing" in the residential property market.

As would be expected, individuals on the front line and those who had been late to the game were the first to be hit by the fallout. These included quick flippers, novice investors, and overstretched homeowners, most of whom had been enticed by the illusory promise of cheap credit and overly optimistic assumptions. Soon, businesses whose fortunes were tied directly to housing, such as real estate agencies, contractors, building materials suppliers, and mortgage brokers, began to see revenues suffer. Many scaled back operations, and some shut their doors completely, adding to the expanding ranks of unemployed homeowners.

A broad range of other industries also felt the ripple effect. Cash-strapped consumers cut back on discretionary purchases like Starbucks's lattes, meals at casual dining restaurants, theme park outings, and movie tickets. The tourism industry, already whacked by high fuel prices and renewed worries over terrorism, saw a drop-off in demand, especially from those at the lower end of the economic spectrum. At the same time, wide swaths of corporate America began to feel the pinch, especially in vulnerable sectors like auto manufacturing, where foreign competitors had already made significant inroads. For industries that had long been forced to offer cheap credit as an inducement for big-ticket purchases, costlier borrowing rates were also becoming a serious threat.

A few observers, according to economist and *New York Times* columnist Paul Krugman, even began to mention the R word—*recession*—while a report from Goldman Sachs noted that the mood of CEOs at the nation's leading companies had slid precipitously. But these and other unsettling developments were merely the early warning signs of the severe economic unraveling that will

drag the United States—and, ultimately, the rest of the world—
into a deep and dark financial abyss, the likes of which haven't
been seen in decades.

By the time the contraction that began in 2006 becomes
full-blown, few individuals, companies, or sectors will escape unscathed. Those struggling on the lowest rungs of the ladder will
almost certainly bear the brunt of the early economic carnage.
With an average of $3,800 in the bank, $2,200 in credit card debt,
a $95,000 mortgage securing a $160,000 home (soon to be worth
far less), and household earnings of approximately $43,000, the
typical American family, as described in the Fed's 2004 consumer
finance survey, won't have a lot of room to maneuver. For those in
more difficult circumstances, like the 10 percent of owners with
zero-to-negative equity in their homes, or the almost 30 percent of
buyers whose mortgages either equal or exceed the value of what
they own, the situation will be especially precarious.

As the downturn spreads, many of the heavily overburdened
will fall behind quickly on mortgage payments and property taxes.
Despite attempts by lenders, through near-term forbearance, to
limit the psychological and bottom-line impact from multiple defaults, record numbers of borrowers will face foreclosure and evic-
tion. Other vulnerable homeowners, like those with so-called affordable mortgages, will be next to go under the economic knife.
Indeed, when the teaser rates on up to $2.5 trillion of adjustable-
rate and option ARMs are reset to market levels prior to 2008, the
size of their mortgage payment adjustments will be shocking, and
many will be unable to meet the new terms. Borrowers who must
pony up additional principal as well as pay higher rates will be
especially hard hit.

Rising mortgage payments won't be the only problem. For
credit-challenged households, higher interest rates will translate
into credit card balances that grow bigger each month. And with
new rules in place, cardholders will have to remit larger minimum
payments than in previous years. Many will be unable to afford

those higher bills and will likely stop paying, adding to the relentless drag on the financial position of banks and other lenders.

Struggling homeowners and low-income consumers will also have to come to terms with hefty fuel and energy costs—for heating and cooling, as well as transportation—equal to more than 6 percent of household spending, based on Commerce Department data. Rising prices for certain key necessities, such as food, household insurance, and medical care, will only make matters worse. Together, the various financial demands will present a daunting challenge for many working Americans, especially those in lower-paid service sector jobs.

For the unemployed, a segment of the population poised to expand rapidly, the outlook will be especially bleak. Few industries will be hiring, while those tied to the property market will scale back sharply.

The pressure to cut or rein in payrolls will come from many fronts. Declining demand, especially for discretionary or big-ticket items, will be at the vanguard. But so will falling margins, as producers that cater to consumers find it increasingly difficult to raise prices enough to compensate for higher input costs. Virtually all businesses will suffer as Americans overall cut spending in favor of repaying debts or replenishing savings amid fading confidence and greater uncertainty about the future.

Ongoing geopolitical developments, including the mounting costs in lives and money in Iraq, as well as increased political discord following the 2006 elections, will likely add to the misery. Even those who seemingly have plenty to spend will hold back, as a contagious wait-to-buy mind-set, one wholly at odds with the hedonistic consumerism of earlier years, begins to spread. Companies and individuals will also be hit with rising taxes and "user fees" of all kinds, because in the early stages, before hard-pressed citizens begin to aggressively fight back, state and local governments will look to fill the gaps caused by falling property values, softening retail sales, and unfunded retirement liabilities.

After a long period of seemingly limitless liquidity, the duo of costlier borrowing and restricted access to credit will become an unexpected burden for even the largest and most resourceful firms. This will occur despite a likely change of course by the Federal Reserve that will push short-term rates lower—though perhaps not as fast as most will hope—after more than two years of monetary policy tightening. In addition, those with funds to lend or invest will almost certainly demand higher-risk premiums than the abnormally low levels offered until mid-2006. Spreads will rebound sharply as uncertainty about the economic outlook and fears over declining credit quality rapidly take hold. Lenders of all kinds will also become far more discriminating under the weight of poor performance, rising loan losses, heightened regulatory scrutiny, and a plethora of negative developments in financial markets, particularly where securitization and derivatives are concerned.

Competition, especially from businesses based overseas, will be more cutthroat than ever, no matter what happens in the foreign exchange markets. Although several factors will likely produce a largely unexpected short-term rebound in the dollar relative to other currencies, which would normally place foreign exporters at a disadvantage, these exporters will almost certainly do what they can to hang on desperately to their U.S. market share.

Needless to say, stock and bond markets will be in turmoil. Under an increasingly debilitating layer of uncertainty, worried CEOs and corporate planners will batten down the hatches in anticipation of tougher times ahead. Those cutbacks will set in motion a vicious circle, where investors decrease equity exposure in sync with newly downgraded expectations, inspiring further caution on Main Street. In addition, investment managers will face pressure from trustees and others whose money they oversee to raise cash to position portfolios as defensively as possible. Unfolding disclosures about the scale of long-term pension and other postretirement obligations, as well as scandals linked to backdated and "spring-loaded" employee stock options, faulty accounting, and instances of outright fraud will further undermine confidence.

As prices fall, speculators and overleveraged speculators will be forced to join those who held out in hopes of selling at the top. So, too, will Wall Street firms, as their risk management models based on value at risk (VaR) spit out ongoing demands for additional sales in the face of increasingly unsettled markets. Over time, the despair on Wall Street will continue to ooze outward, further souring the mood in boardrooms and executive suites around the country. Businesses that had been kept alive only by virtue of stable markets and ample liquidity will not cope well with more hostile circumstances as end demand steadily erodes. Many will also discover that access to capital of any kind—cheap or otherwise—has seemingly vanished overnight, limiting their ability to respond to fast-changing circumstances and long-range operating requirements.

Eventually, individuals with plenty of resources at their disposal will also begin to cut back, as portfolios bleed with losses in various asset classes. Even luxury goods makers and providers of high-end services will be hurt by the broad retrenchment, as the wealthy shy away from conspicuous consumption in the face of growing public resentment. Month after month, the U.S. unemployment rate will increase, eating away at overall demand in a self-perpetuating vicious circle. As firms continue to respond by slashing jobs, benefits, and wages, relations between management and workers will become ever more strained. Confrontations will be widespread, and calls for strikes and other aggressive responses will increase, especially in industries where unions still retain some measure of their historic influence.

In no time at all, the economic malaise will spread throughout the domestic economy and, by way of various trade links, international financial markets and other nodes of globalization to the rest of the world. Hardest hit initially will be countries that depend on the free-spending ways of the overburdened American consumer. They will be the same nations that accumulated massive reserves of dollars and holdings of U.S. assets in an expensive yet ultimately failed strategy to maintain an export market for their rapidly expanding output.

With prices in the property market under severe pressure because of sharply rising defaults, a relentless credit bottleneck, and surging volatility in various stock, bond, commodity, and derivative markets, the financial system will seem under siege. Adding to the sense of foreboding will be a mad rush by speculators and banks scrambling to unload illiquid and risky positions. Evidence of sizable and dangerous cracks will appear in the financial landscape. And then the inevitable will happen.

6

SYSTEMIC
CRISIS

"Rashness brings success to few, misfortune to many."
—Phaedrus

When long lines formed at American gas stations in the summer of 1979, most people believed they were caused by a shortage of fuel. In reality, notes John Sterman, a professor at Massachusetts Institute of Technology and author of *Business Dynamics: Systems Thinking and Modeling for a Complex World,* "The total inventory of gas in the system remained nearly constant. But the actions of nervous drivers moved the gas from below-ground tanks at the corner gas stations to above-ground rolling storage"—vehicle fuel tanks, in other words. The amount in question: two-and-a-half days' supply. Thus, while many Americans blamed OPEC and President Carter, the fear and panic that arose when drivers saw cars queuing to fill up and prices moving higher at the pump actually played a major role in stoking the crisis.

No doubt a systemic meltdown will provoke a similar response. For the financial system and the markets, however, the fallout will likely be worse than any downturn in many decades, owing to a unique combination of modern developments and incendiary circumstances. The explosive growth of derivatives trading and leveraged hedge fund investing, hidden behind a shroud of lightly regulated secrecy, means that few people will have a handle on where dangerous risk is concentrated or overall levels of exposure—not until it's too late. At the same time, a long period of benign economic conditions, a multiyear decline in risk premiums, and the illusion that regulators are on top of everything will sow a mixture of complacency, confusion, and cognitive dissonance.

Simply put, people will find it difficult to react in a timely, logical, or focused fashion to the unfolding calamity. In fact, many will be out of kilter from the very start. Even the Federal Reserve, which long ago acquired the seemingly unrelenting habit of putting out economic and financial forest fires by turning on the monetary liquidity spigot full blast, will likely fail to come to grips with the disaster. And if it does realize what is occurring, its response will be uncharacteristic, to say the least.

After a long span enabling credit and various other bubbles, odds are high that the Fed will suddenly get what might be referred to as central bank "religion" and adopt a substantial measure of restraint, ironically perhaps, at just the wrong time. Spurred by worries about the impact that aggressive monetary easing will have on inflation expectations, domestic capital markets, and the dollar, and compelled to resume the long-abandoned role of hard-nosed central bankers after Alan Greenspan's legacy of "printing" money, the Fed is likely to underreact to the brewing crisis.

Moreover, members of the Federal Reserve, like others inside and outside of government, will almost certainly not have a clear strategy. Despite increased levels of sophistication and the broad use of modern risk management systems, no one can be sure how new or exotic instruments and markets will behave when conditions take an ominous turn. The sheer scale of the unfolding financial crisis—in terms of the number of participants, firms, regulators, products, countries, and markets—will make it difficult to penetrate the problems. Instead, complexity, unfamiliarity, uncertainty, misplaced complacency, and newfound prudence will trigger a broadly reactive response—the kind that has fostered numerous panics, bank runs, and market crashes through the years.

This time, however, a vast and efficient global communications network will ensure that destructive energies are rapidly transmitted to billions of people. So, too, will trading technology that facilitates and encourages traders and investors to act on their impulses. Many will find it too easy to shoot first—or point and click—and ask questions later in a 21st-century rush for the exits. Not only will the fastest or sharpest operators look to get out. Firms that have come to depend on leverage, including hedge funds, brokers, and even banks, will also face immediate and rapidly growing pressure to scale back positions because of demands for additional cash collateral or reduced access to financing. Meanwhile, those who still have the wherewithal to initiate fresh positions or act independently will look to dive in and take advantage of the stampede.

Eventually, the combination of unwinding and retrenchment by Wall Street dealers looking to cut back dramatically on price-making activities will weigh on market liquidity. Volumes will dry up in many trading arenas, and dealing spreads will widen considerably or even disappear. That will provoke even more fear and uncertainty, as participants react to the prospect of not getting out at all if they don't act quickly or forcefully. As the old trading saw goes, the first cut is usually the cheapest—after that, it is likely to be hara-kiri.

Initially, those who are exposed will seek to unload the largest, most dangerous, or least valuable positions. As the loss-cutting crowd expands, the upheaval will seep through into more liquid markets. Mostly, the pressure will be felt on the downside. Nonetheless, following the dramatic expansion of complex arbitrage, derivative, and relative value positions accumulated over several years, many markets will also see abrupt and violent squeezes to the upside. Firms with massive bets on a fall in the greenback, for example, could be stung by a widespread scramble to unwind similar positions. This will likely be spurred by a short-term rush for traditional safe-haven investments, an unusually unaccommodating Fed, and a scramble to raise U.S. currency as bankers hurriedly call in outstanding dollar-denominated loans.

Others will swing wildly up and down, stirred by skittishness or because of urgent demands for cash or collateral. With prices disappearing and volume surging in some markets and drying up in others, minute-by-minute trading conditions will deteriorate even further. By then, individuals and markets will buckle under the acute stress, exacerbating the growing sense of panic. The widespread use of similar risk management approaches certainly won't help matters, because many firms will be operating dangerously in sync with one another as conditions worsen. Most will look to cut risk relative to capital, while those that depend on leverage will likely be raising cash to meet margin calls.

The far-reaching multiyear shift by Wall Street into financial activities that involve market-based valuations will also boost anxiety. These include proprietary trading and securitization, which transformed many formerly illiquid—thus, difficult to value—obligations such as mortgages into marketable securities. "In a time of panic," noted Henry Kaufman, president of Henry Kaufman & Company, Inc., and a former research director for Salomon Brothers, "The last thing in the world you want to focus on is price."

A close-knit relationship network, where traders quickly pass along rumors and tips, will compound the negatively charged atmosphere. Many hedge fund managers are connected in one way or another, often because they were former colleagues at other firms or investment banks.

Inherently flawed models that depend on rational pricing and normal volatility patterns to gauge risk will not function as expected. In fact, more than a few will be thrown totally out of whack, leaving some firms with dangerous exposure that will be difficult to measure or manage. Historically, correlations among securities, sectors, and asset classes tend to change, sometimes abruptly, when markets are in turmoil. When that happens, the process of identifying potentially catastrophic threats and coping with the intense demands of active portfolio management will become still more difficult. Moreover, during a crisis, pricing becomes increasingly nonlinear; instead of moving in relatively continuous incremental steps, prices jump abruptly higher and lower, often without warning.

Unfortunately, all of these unfamiliar and unusual circumstances will follow years of relative calm, when deficient risk management approaches and intense competition to justify high fees encouraged a piling-on of risks in many markets. With each passing day, the pressure for ever more unwinding of money-losing positions by an expanding circle of financial operators will grow. Others outside of Wall Street will also join the rush. Nervous individuals and institutions with a newfound aversion to risk will scale back exposure. Corporate America will put deals and spending plans on hold, rattled by unsettled markets and admonitions from investors.

At the same time, a growing list of scandals and the fallout from the change in retirement accounting standards will add to rising public hostility toward both Wall Street and Main Street.

As activity in some trading arenas surges, markets will see technical glitches and breakdowns similar to those that occurred in Japan during January of 2006. Mobile phone and point-and-click panic selling by individual investors after a scandal at high-flyer Livedoor forced an unprecedented early shutdown of the Tokyo Stock Exchange, the world's second-largest equity market. With liquidity and access to borrowed money evaporating, a broad range of stock, bond, and commodity markets in turmoil, and investors and lenders desperately trying to cut losses and reduce risk, the stage will be set for something to give.

It is always hard to know ahead of time which catalyst will light the fuse. Past upheavals have been difficult to pin down to one cause. Often, an accumulation of little sparks causes a spontaneous eruption. Still, the trigger for a full-fledged systemic crisis will likely be the abrupt and unexpected failure of an aggressive financial operator. That could mean a multibillion-dollar hedge fund, with a large and highly leveraged exposure to certain illiquid markets or exotic securities, or a private equity firm saddled with debt but with little in the way of marketable assets.

At that point, the wide-eyed delusions of yet another new era will be revealed as age-old fallacies.

Allegedly sophisticated operators will suddenly discover that swapping safe, liquid, and relatively straightforward investments for risky, illiquid, and utterly complex positions is not clever arbitrage but a value-destroying proposition. Many will also learn the hard way that accurate pricing, access to market liquidity, the cost and availability of credit, and the viability of the entire financial system ultimately depend on a kind of collective faith. They will realize that when risk is mixed and matched in unfamiliar combinations—traded, shifted or sliced and diced, or repackaged into bigger or smaller pieces and sold off—the potential for destructive blowback doesn't leave the system. Nor does it create lots of extra room for everyone to take on more risk, a point that so many will have missed.

As for popular risk management theories, the smart money will recognize belatedly that it is not a good idea to be part of a large crowd holding similar positions looking for greater fools to sell to when the time comes to bail out, like those who relied on portfolio insurance prior to the 1987 stock market crash. Finally, many will fully understand what Nigel Jenkinson, a director of the Bank of England, meant when he said in the spring of 2006, "There is a dark side connected to financial integration. If shocks are large enough, the financial system becomes a risk transmitter rather than a risk disburser."

Helping to accelerate the spreading global contagion will be the presence of large international firms that had been speculating and engaging in arbitrage across borders and markets. This will also ensure—until things break down completely—that systemic strains and stresses are transmitted everywhere and anywhere, virtually at the speed of light. A constant global ripple effect will occur as positions are adjusted to take account of risk management strategies or cash-raising demands. The widespread use of flawed models will further aggravate the situation.

Rather than hedging specific positions with related transactions, under modern risk management regimes, firms adjust exposure at the portfolio level. That means a bad trade in an arcane and thinly traded currency derivative could potentially be offset by the sale of British government bonds, the purchase of gold futures, or the liquidation of a diverse portfolio of international stocks. In an expansive systemic crisis, however, such an approach will leave many large operators even more vulnerable, in danger of being blindsided by an unforeseen turn of events. That risk will almost certainty be accentuated by back-office systems that have failed to keep pace with the parabolic rise in volumes.

Whether most firms adequately hedge their exposure, the pervasive and excessive use of leverage and the perilous illusions of 21st-century finance mean that lenders will very quickly become very cautious. Banks, for instance, will scramble to call in loans or raise "haircuts," boosting the amount of collateral required to secure the amounts financed. So will prime brokers—Wall Street dealers that have played a pivotal role in underwriting the vast expansion of the hedge fund sector. Indeed, their history as financiers of illiquidity will likely place them at the center of the next phase of the crisis, when destabilizing conditions will force many firms to shut their doors, leading to more of the same.

By the time the systemic crisis is full-blown, there will almost certainly have been a domino-like collapse of more than a few large intermediaries and allegedly sophisticated global financial firms, including hedge funds, insurers, and brokers. As the number of failures grows, concerns over counterparty risk will take center stage. Lenders, investors, and risk managers will fret and gossip about which institution is next. Worries about fraud and chicanery will boost anxiety to a fever pitch. Even firms not in dire straits may suddenly find themselves at risk. In times of upheaval, a lack of information and concern about the ability of others to manage their exposure often spurs a self-fulfilling prophecy, where idle chatter alone leads to institutions being squeezed or cut off—just when they need access to financing most.

Individuals and institutions won't just worry about losing money; they will also be concerned about having access to enough funds to meet day-to-day operating needs. When financial institutions are in trouble, especially those whose obligations aren't covered by the FDIC safety net, legal or accounting issues can limit the size and extent of customer withdrawals, including those not categorized as general obligations of the firm. More than six months after commodity broker Refco went bankrupt in October 2005 amid allegations of fraud, the *New York Post* reported that 7,000 clients had been unable to withdraw their money because their accounts had been frozen by the courts.

With fear and uncertainty on the rise, people will invariably worsen the problem by hoarding cash and other resources, much as those panicky car and truck drivers topped off their gas tanks in the late 1970s. The mood will turn increasingly sour, and conditions in and out of the financial markets will deteriorate further. People will overreact and refrain from initiating or following through on even routine transactions and economic activities, as they seek shelter from the unknown. In part, their responses will stem from what can best be described as a lack of coordination— not knowing what others will do and thus assuming the worst. Historically, such reactions are often seen in situations involving what economists call "Knightian uncertainty," that is, where the risks are impossible to measure.

Based on the reported behavior of some firms that were involved—and, interestingly enough, financially at risk—in the 1998 Federal Reserve–led rescue of Long Term Capital Management, it seems a good bet that more than a few operators will take an entirely self-serving view of any turmoil. They will fan the flames of other firms' misfortune or otherwise exacerbate the woes of weak institutions by arbitrarily withdrawing financial or other support. Or they will "front-run," or step ahead of efforts to stem the bleeding, hoping to force capitulation by at-risk firms from which they then can profit.

Eventually, the crisis will reach a fever pitch when lenders, especially key suppliers of funds, become unhinged by the gridlock and panic. Many of those institutions will in turn face an abrupt, unexpected struggle for their own survival. Paradoxically, those at the center of the credit-creation process generally operate with far more leverage than do the firms to which they lend. Soon, reports will circulate that smaller financial institutions are shutting their doors, and rumors will begin to surface that a major commercial or investment bank, or one of the government-sponsored enterprises, is facing "liquidity problems."

Bank failures have been a recurring feature of the American financial landscape since the nation's founding. Although historically low interest rates and a benign operating environment have been something of a godsend since the equity bubble burst, circumstances have not always been so fortuitous. In past decades, economic contractions, industry changes, incompetence, and, most important, greed, notes Irvine Sprague, former chair and director of the FDIC, have forced many lenders to shut their doors. Two years after the 1991 recession ended, more than a hundred banks failed, according to Roger Ferguson, former vice chair of the Federal Reserve, while in the last three years of the 1980s, more than 200 such institutions on average went bust every year, not including the large number of S&Ls that also shut down.

The real fear is that one or more of the large intermediaries that play a critical role in the nation's financial infrastructure will find themselves in hot water. Most people believe that the too-big-to-fail doctrine will invariably come into play, despite legislation such as FDICIA and politically unrealistic bluster that Washington would be willing to walk away from such a development. In all likelihood, that theory will be severely tested. With concentrated exposure to real estate, derivatives, and leveraged speculation, and their reliance on risk management approaches that will fall short when markets are under siege, numerous major financial institutions are likely to fail catastrophically.

Even a modest hiccup in the functioning of the banking system and modern financial infrastructure will likely cause chaos and a dangerous secondary chain reaction that would be difficult to stop. Perhaps anticipating such an event, the U.S. Bond Market Association announced in early 2006 that it would lead an initiative to set up a standby "bank" that the Federal Reserve would activate if one of the two clearing banks in the U.S. government securities markets was "suddenly forced to leave the business."

Unfortunately, those counting on regulators or the political establishment to come to the rescue when the financial system unravels will find little solace. Historically, government officials have either been too slow or too fast to react to unfolding crises because of lobbying, conflicts of interest, and a culture that abhors true leadership and anticipatory decision making. There are some exceptions, of course. During the Long Term Capital Management debacle, the New York Fed chief reportedly gathered everyone into a room and read them the riot act, which arguably nipped a looming financial disaster in the bud. This time, though, the scale of the crisis will be far greater and will enmesh a mind-boggling array of individuals, firms, markets, jurisdictions, and regulatory authorities around the globe, at least some of which will have no interest in cooperating.

Numerous activities and participants will also be beyond the reach of any competent jurisdiction or regulatory overseer, further diminishing the prospect of a coordinated solution to a multifaceted and fast-unfolding financial meltdown, despite some attempts at forward planning. During the spring of 2006, Europe's financial regulators held a "war games exercise" to address cross-border issues that might arise following the failure of a major operator in one of the member countries. In September, New York Fed president Timothy Geithner, SEC commissioner Annette Nazareth, and the head of the United Kingdom's Financial Services Authority wrote in the *Financial Times* that "[i]n a more integrated global market, we will increasingly find ourselves compelled to pursue borderless solutions." Unfortunately, although such efforts could prove of value, history suggests otherwise. Just consider the example of the lack of jurisdictional coordination that hampered rescue efforts in the wake of 2005's Hurricane Katrina disaster.

Indeed, because of the multiplicity of risks, markets, and counterparties involved, the situation might be akin to the disastrous forest fires that swept across the West Coast of the United States in recent decades. Often, there were simply too many hot spots to tackle at once, and wide swaths were left ablaze until they eventually burned themselves out.

Few areas of the financial system will be unaffected when the meltdown rages. In the insurance sector, for example, debt downgrades and defaults will occur at a quickening pace. That will leave individuals, companies, and governments dangerously exposed and add to the financial tsunami that will already have swamped the municipal bond and asset-backed securities markets. Other intermediaries will also discover that doubts about their survival can quickly become self-fulfilling. Individuals and businesses will withdraw cash or hurriedly transfer funds to the dwindling universe of institutions deemed safe, while wholesale suppliers of equity or borrowed money will be even quicker to turn off the tap. At least some of the $2 trillion held in money market funds will anxiously flee to safer pastures as the prices of one or more pools fall below par— "breaks the buck"—because of shaky markets and short-maturity holdings that turn out to be riskier than expected.

While Wall Street continues to seize up, the long-predicted tectonic shift in global imbalances will put pressure on spending, investment, and growth. Soon, the rapidly expanding loss of confidence in the financial system will completely overwhelm any remaining strength in the real economy. By then, the next phase of unraveling will be underway.

7

DEPRESSION

"It's a recession when your neighbor loses his job;
it's a depression when you lose yours."

President Harry S. Truman

In his 1968 book *Social Theory and Social Structure*, sociologist Robert K. Merton wrote about what took place at a fictional institution, The Last National Bank, when a large number of customers happened to arrive at once. Even though the lender was honest and well run, the sudden—but inexplicable—presence of long lines caused considerable consternation. That eventually triggered fears and rumors about the bank's financial health, spurring uneasy customers to rush in and withdraw their money. Like most banks, however, Last National had loaned out the bulk of depositors' cash, keeping only a small fraction on hand to meet day-to-day liquidity needs. As a result, the surge of withdrawals precipitated what Merton described as a self-fulfilling crisis, forcing an essentially healthy institution into insolvency.

History suggests that emotion and psychology indeed play an important role in matters of money. When consumers are optimistic about the future, they feel inclined to spend or borrow more than they otherwise might. In contrast, if they are worried about their job or their bills, their pessimism can have a deleterious effect. They will cut back on unnecessary purchases and boost savings in hopes of giving themselves extra breathing room in case things don't work out.

When enough people lean in any one direction, the impact can be striking, especially if initial economic conditions mirror existing sentiment. In the early 1980s, when interest rates soared into the double digits and the economy slid into deep recession, fearful consumers cut back sharply on spending and borrowing. That pushed the personal savings rate to near 10 percent. Then, aided by a dramatic about-face in monetary policy, attitudes changed. The University of Michigan consumer sentiment index rose from 65.4 in mid-1982 to 100.1 in January 1984. The rebound matched similar increases in new home starts, auto sales, and other key economic indicators, as well as growth in household debt levels.

By 2006, circumstances were dramatically different—and the economic pendulum was poised to swing back sharply in the opposite direction. So, too, was consumer sentiment, which had remained upbeat for a long time, despite the bursting equity bubble and the brief slowdown in 2001. In large part, Americans had found it easy to stick to their optimistic guns because they had not experienced a wrenching recession for more than 15 years. As a consequence, however, many were totally unprepared for tough times, both mentally and in terms of the resources they had at their disposal. Household borrowing and debt service payments as a percentage of disposable income had reached record highs nearly six years after the equity bubble had burst. The savings rate had also dipped solidly into the red, historically a very rare phenomenon.

In many respects, the mood in early 2006 was akin to the optimism that existed in the immediate aftermath of the 1929 stock market crash—just before the economy fell into a multiyear tailspin. As *BusinessWeek* noted in a look-back feature article, "The horror of [that] period was heightened by [the] failure of most Americans, in the early months, to realize how bad it would be."

No doubt similar rude awakenings will occur as the first phase of the coming financial and economic disaster begins to unfold, thanks to incoherence and incompetence in Washington and an unexpectedly restrained and increasingly out-of-touch Federal Reserve. The growth of securitization, an increasing reliance on variable-rate financing, the shift away from defined-benefit pensions, the rise of outsourcing and the service-based economy, the 2005 Bankruptcy Reform Act, and other developments will ensure that ordinary Americans bear the full brunt of the pain as the economy crumbles.

Also, a vast array of public and private sector obligations and contingent liabilities, many of which will ultimately be unpaid, will put the kibosh on spending. People will learn the hard way that many safety nets are no longer available. In fact, the pressure from rapidly expanding budget deficits and falling tax revenues, combined with the alarming cost of retirement-related promises, will force every level of government to scale back public assistance just when it is needed most. The programs that remain in place won't offer enough to help the needy keep pace with the actual costs of survival or assist everyone who needs help.

The squeeze will be so severe that many municipalities will have a hard time even staying afloat. That situation is likely to be exacerbated by the substantial impact of years of infrastructure neglect. The American Society of Civil Engineers estimated in a 2005 "report card" that the nation's five-year infrastructure investment need had reached an alarming $1.6 trillion. Hardest hit, of course, will be state and local government authorities, such as school districts, that depend in large part on revenues from property taxes. Public services will also suffer, as police officers, firefighters, teachers, and others are laid off amid widespread budget cutting.

Undoubtedly, the collapsing real estate market will inspire a lucid and widespread awareness of a harsh new reality. In the decade before 2006, according to the Center for Economic and Policy Research, the ballooning property market created more than $5 trillion of so-called bubble wealth, equivalent to nearly

40 percent of gross domestic product—with debts to go with it. Yet when prices fall, those debts—as well as all the others accumulated through the years—will remain. That level of outstanding debt will exacerbate an unprecedented plunge in spending and will eventually result in widespread defaults and bankruptcies.

Persistent asset liquidations and crashing stock, bond, and commodity markets—with the exception, perhaps, of oil and other petroleum-related products—will only add to the misery, either directly or in terms of their depressing psychological impact.

In the initial stage of the dark period ahead, the wealth effect will shift violently into reverse after a long and relatively uninterrupted upswing, even after taking account of the bursting of the 1990's equity bubble. Americans' willingness to buy or borrow, except out of necessity or desperation, will diminish rapidly on increasingly dire news about the state of the financial system and the economy, not to mention their own deteriorating household finances. Unemployment will skyrocket as both large and small firms react to crumbling domestic demand. With consumers accounting for around three-quarters of overall U.S. spending, few businesses will be able to resist the pressure to slash and burn jobs and expenses in anticipation of continued bad times.

Firms that benefit from discretionary purchases, particularly those in leisure-related industries, will likely be slammed hard in the early stages of the downswing. Their misfortunes will be due not only to the ranks of Americans who cannot afford to spend but also to those who still have money and who will avoid the conspicuous consumption limelight. Domestic service providers will also suffer markedly from the effects of a rapidly cooling economy. However, faltering demand and brutal competition from overseas producers will depress prices and profits on manufactured goods as well, especially those that are somewhat commoditized. In this environment, a deflationary mind-set will spread like wildfire, making the economic situation more worrisome by the day.

Whether out of choice or not, prospective buyers will adopt an indifferent or even an aggressive stance in regard to how and when they spend their money. Many consumers will try to haggle over the cost of anything and everything. Purchasers will make ridiculous offers, dramatically undercutting listed prices. Unfortunately, because of the expanding universe of sellers, that will prove to be exactly the right strategy. Attitudes about buying new items and expectations about the length of the replacement cycle will undergo a dramatic turnabout, reverting to the more cautious stance of less carefree times.

Ironically, relentless quality improvements, once featured as key selling points in stores and showrooms, will be put to the test during the initial downward turn. Many former serial buyers of consumer goods will suddenly decide to stick with old but still-functioning vehicles, electronics, furniture, and machinery instead of trading up for new and improved models. Many people will adopt a relatively inflexible wait-and-see attitude, figuring it will be better to hold off on purchasing anything until prices drop. Their caution will add to ongoing declines in prices, revenues, and margins, forcing businesses to scale back spending and investment plans even further.

For those who don't have much money, bartering for food, shelter, or other necessities in exchange for heirlooms, furnishings, and, of course, labor, may be the only option when jobs, charity, and public assistance are increasingly scarce or nonexistent. Sadly, some Americans may have no choice other than to go without. Across the nation, hunger, poverty, and homelessness will rise in measured lockstep with a surging unemployment rate. At the same time, the long-growing divide between rich and poor will continue to widen, though the numbers that make up the former group will shrink by the day.

A shortage of cash and the willingness to wait, along with a host of other economic and systemic pressures, will depress virtually all collectible, commodity, and asset markets, especially where legions of overleveraged owners have been transformed into panicky liquidators. Already in freefall, real estate turnover will drop to almost zero, as residential and commercial property buyers either walk away or decide that avoiding major decisions is the prudent course of action.

Eventually, distressed and overextended investors, speculators, and owners will slash prices and leapfrog over each other in a race to the bottom, forced to compete against an ever-expanding supply of abandoned or foreclosed properties while potential buyers all but disappear. Over time, absolute or no-reserve auctions will displace traditional marketing approaches, as those who must get out are forced to take aggressive action to stem losses and prevent liabilities from spiraling totally out of control.

As financial woes mount, people will hunt for wrongdoers and will likely find no shortage of prospective miscreants. In fact, splintering asset markets will likely reveal chasms filled with evidence of chicanery and misappropriation. No doubt many schemes will have stemmed from bogus appraisals and valuations that were skewed by blatant conflicts of interest during the bubble years. The domino-like failures of numerous hedge funds, insurers, brokers, and other financial intermediaries because of incompetence, greed, or fraud will inspire outrage. Where money is concerned, people will be in no mood to forgive or forget, instead feeling a growing desire for revenge.

Even where no explicit crime or impropriety seems to have taken place, individuals and companies that can afford it will attempt to use the legal system to extricate themselves from deals and potentially costly commitments agreed to during times of unbridled optimism. The nation's courts will be buried under a deluge of filings and lawsuits, raising serious doubts about prospective legal exposure and spurring those who are potentially vulnerable to be even more cautious about planning for the future. The criminal justice system will also creak under the weight of a sharp increase in arrests, trials, and incarcerations, as crimes against people and property soar and evidence of past illegalities surfaces.

Along with individuals and state and local governments, many businesses will also find themselves in desperate financial straits.

The smaller the firm and the fewer advantages and resources it has at its disposal, the more likely its eventual failure. But larger enterprises, especially those that have come to depend on faded brands, munificent investors and lenders, or momentum based on size alone, won't be immune. Eventually, the American landscape will be littered with the wreckage of what were once seen as the bluest of blue chips. They will be joined by casualties from the post-1990's boom in private equity and leveraged buyouts. Saddled with gargantuan loads of debt and bled by dealmakers and bankers with little or no regard for long-run viability, hundreds of companies will quickly crumble when ultrathin margins of error are easily exceeded.

Unfortunately, few will have the support of those who helped put them there. Banks and other key stakeholders might once have had a vested or moral interest in helping troubled businesses to turn around their operations but not this time. Instead, the rise of securitized financing and the pervasive influence of hard-nosed—and frequently short-sighted—operators like hedge funds means that many key players won't care about the collateral damage that a failed business causes. Instead of working things out, the mantra will be cut and run. For some of the new breed of financiers, there will be little choice—they, too, will be struggling to survive.

Commercial banks will have their own problems. No matter how fast they raise fees, call in loans, tighten lending standards, sell assets, and restructure balance sheets, many will nevertheless be seriously caught out by years of complacency and risky activities. Whether their problems stem from borrowing short and lending long, relying on shaky liabilities to finance illiquid investments, betting the ranch on derivatives or the real estate sector, or engaging in the sort of leveraged speculation that bankers once abhorred, thousands of financial institutions will inevitably face a terrible moment of truth. They will hit a fissure in the road that hundreds—or more likely thousands—won't get past. Insurers, brokers, investment advisors, mutual fund groups, and other financial operators will also see their numbers ravaged by restructuring and bankruptcy.

Initially, many Americans will feel reassured that their checking and savings accounts are backed by federal deposit insurance. Over time, the failure of more and more banks is likely to weigh on confidence and boost anxiety. Spurred by job losses and personal hardships, as well as by gloomy reports and emotionally charged rumors, people will increasingly worry if their funds are at risk. As a consequence, even some prudently managed institutions will end up with the same fate as the fictional Last National Bank.

In an environment where millions are suffering and fear runs rampant, the social mood will turn ugly. Conflicts and violent confrontations between managers and employees, the wealthy and the poor, the working and the unemployed, and other haves and have-nots will become commonplace. Rising alcoholism, drug abuse, and domestic violence on the heels of stress and persistent money woes will help tear the economic and social fabric even further apart. There will be a hunt for scapegoats—in Washington, in the media, and even in the streets. Those with losses or other grievances will cast about widely and openly for people to blame, whether or not they are directly responsible.

Some of those cast adrift by the collapse will want to move on rather than focus on why or who is at fault. Unfortunately, no small number will realize rather quickly that they might not be able to escape the morass. Many of those who lose their job and are in debt, or who find themselves upside-down on their mortgages and dunned for escalating payments, or who were blindsided by illness or another uninsured calamity won't have the option of a "fresh start," especially after 2005's so-called bankruptcy reforms. Instead, at least some Americans in serious financial hot water will delay filing for bankruptcy until virtually all hope is lost. Others will have a tough time even finding legal counsel willing to represent their interests in bankruptcy court because of new reporting requirements, increased paperwork, and other limitations.

With onerous rules designed to force all but the most impoverished petitioners to repay their debts over a five-year period—even if they lack enough money to survive—the financial recovery that would normally follow a dramatic shakeout will be constrained, as liquidity and confidence return more slowly to the economy than before.

In spite of rule changes, the financial sector will face the devastating fallout of years of shoddy lending practices, excessive risk taking, and blatant mismanagement. Most likely, the early casualties will be smaller institutions and aggressive thrifts. Over time, however, the numbers will add up, more than matching the extraordinary totals last seen during the Great Depression. In just under a year, from October 1930 through July 1931, nearly 1,400 banks failed, accounting for around 2 percent of the nation's deposits, according to economist Milton Friedman. During a second wave, from August 1931 to January 1932, a total of 1,860 financial institutions failed.

Reports of banks shutting their doors won't have much impact at first, though growing numbers of individuals, especially older Americans, will almost certainly shift their funds into accounts at the largest institutions. When news eventually hits, however, that one or more of the better-known firms is on the rocks, relative complacency will give way to serious concern and a broad loss of confidence, despite reassurances from Wall Street, politicians, the media, and the regulatory establishment. People will rush to hoard cash, and some will begin aggressively to accumulate precious metals, while sales of security systems, safes, and guns will rapidly gain pace.

Groaning under the weight of multiple investigations, a spate of high-profile criminal and civil trials, myriad congressional and agency hearings, and an acrimonious political standoff, Washington will be of little help in stemming the rising tide of panic and fear. Pressure for the government to "do something" to solve the mushrooming financial and economic crisis will bring forth only tough talk and an epidemic of populist proposals, many of which will be targeted at immigrants and foreigners. Calls for sharply higher tariffs, citizen identity cards, and massive walled borders will dominate the agenda. Not surprisingly, other nations will respond in kind, threatening economic and political retaliation and abandonment of the United States and its interests. In the Mideast, Latin America, and other volatile regions around the world, there will be talk of embargoes and war.

Eventually, with a decades-long orgy of credit expansion unraveling fast; the meltdown of stock, bond, commodity, and other markets; a cratering economy; and more of the nation's largest financial institutions precariously on the edge, the Federal Reserve and Washington as a whole will have reached a critical juncture. There will be widespread pressure, bordering perhaps on hysteria, for somebody, somewhere to take action and stem the rapidly rising tide of disaster.

Only then, after being unwilling to react quickly and forcefully enough early on, the Federal Reserve will abruptly shift gears, no longer fearing the consequences of an aggressive monetary response. In a sense, they will have nothing to lose. With immediate effect, they will give up their self-imposed yoke of restraint and move wholeheartedly into money-creation mode. That will mark the beginning of the second phase of the great unraveling.

8

HYPERINFLATION

"I will print money today so that people can survive."
—Robert Mugabe

In the spring of 2006, the *New York Times* reported that rampant inflation in the African nation of Zimbabwe had boosted the effective cost of a single sheet of two-ply toilet paper to Z$417. That price was not far below the value of the Zimbabwean Z$500 bill, the smallest in circulation, "spawning jokes about an impending better use" for the currency, said the *Times*. Another article in the *Times* (London) noted that with the Z$50,000 banknote being the largest available denomination—to avoid causing inflation, according to President Mugabe—paying for a taxi fare could take almost as long as the journey itself, while the demand for imported heavy-duty cash-counting machines remained strong despite deteriorating economic conditions.

Such is a world beset by hyperinflation, where monthly or even daily price changes can hit double- and triple-digit percentages, eventually rendering the currency all but worthless. In such a surreal time, the average citizen is left stunned and fearful about what tomorrow will bring. People who have worked hard, saved plenty, and lived frugally end up impoverished and desperate. Ironically, those imbued with a hedonistic, live-for-today approach occasionally have the last laugh.

History offers up many instances when inflation was allowed, or even encouraged, to rise at a meteoric pace, often as a way of supporting failed policies and despotic regimes. In ancient Rome, for example, coins containing gold or silver were sometimes shaved, counterfeited, or debased in some other way to increase, as if by magic, the funds available to wage war and pay for a broad range of government extravagances.

Eventually, the need for a more convenient, efficient, and secure medium of exchange than specie, as commodity-based coinage is called, promulgated the creation of paper currency that was directly convertible into a hard asset, most often gold or silver. Through the years, however, under constant pressure to placate supporters and satisfy the insatiable demands of an often fickle citizenry, many countries have broken that link. In August 1971, President Nixon faced an array of economic woes and a corresponding outward flow of gold as anxious nonresidents and foreign central banks cashed in their dollars. He decreed that American currency could no longer be exchanged into the yellow metal. In one fell swoop, the greenback was transformed from a store of value into nothing more than a promise, a piece of paper with ink on it. As such, it was an obligation that few governments with printing presses at their disposal—or their equivalent—would ever honor in full.

With the widespread adoption of unbacked paper, or "fiat" currencies, nations such as Germany, Hungary, Yugoslavia, Bolivia, Brazil, Argentina, and, of course, Zimbabwe have at times been able to employ a less labor-intensive approach than the Romans to boost the total amount of money in circulation. They have simply churned out more of the stuff—a lot more. On those occasions, it has literally been a case of cranking up the presses, machines located at official government-run facilities or operated by high-volume subcontractors in other countries. At the height of hyperinflation during 1923 in Weimar Germany, 150 printing companies reportedly had 2,000 presses operating around the clock producing deutsch marks. When inflation reaches astronomical levels that strain existing capabilities, governments have resorted to imaginative workarounds, like printing on only one side of the paper or stamping extra zeros on older, smaller-denomination notes. Occasionally, resourceful nations have even allowed currency surreptitiously created by counterfeiters to be converted into the real thing ex post facto, in a kind of private-public partnership.

Nowadays, digital technology, credit and debit cards, fractional-reserve banking, and the legal authority typically granted to central banks or other monetary authorities make it easy for governments to boost the money supply more or less at will. And if need be, they can do so quickly and for any amount, without short-term worry about whether enough ink, paper, or machine time is available.

Using a simple example, modern-day money creation generally kicks off when a monetary authority decides to purchase an asset, typically a government obligation such as bill or a bond, in the open market. Then, when the settlement date arrives, the buyer credits the seller's bank account with the amount due. Where do the funds come from? Essentially, they are bookkeeping entries created out of thin air.

After the "credit money" enters the system, it is transformed once again through the wonders of fractional-reserve banking. As with the example of The Last National Bank cited in Chapter 7, only a small percentage of the funds held on deposit remain immediately accessible. In most cases, official policy dictates the amount that needs to be set aside to satisfy withdrawal requests. Balances above regulatory minimums are either lent or invested, boosting the bank accounts of other borrowers and investors or repeating the credit-pyramiding process. Successive rounds of this activity create a virtual circle of money supply growth, otherwise known as the multiplier effect.

In the United States, the minimum reserve requirement (MRR) is 10 percent for demand deposits such as checking accounts. Once an account is credited with $1 million, the financial institution involved can turn around, take the $900,000 above

MRR, and put the money to work as it sees fit. When those funds are eventually recycled by other intermediaries, the quantity of new money in circulation in the form of credit increases by another $810,000, or $900,000 less 10 percent, and so on and so forth, until the original $1 million eventually becomes $10 million.

Even nowadays, few economies function without at least some physical currency in circulation, so a bank can arrange to have its account at the monetary authority debited in exchange for notes and coins. The problem is that without an anchor in the form of a relatively rare asset, the only limit to the amount of credit-based money that can be created is what official policy or prudence dictates. The process is not self-correcting in any normal sense of the word. In an economy with a "gold standard" currency, however, hemorrhaging reserves of the yellow metal act as a natural brake on bad economic behavior by the government.

When a fiat currency's empty promises are in play, monetary and economic stability depend on more than policymakers' wisdom and stewardship. Politicians, bureaucrats, and other officials must also be willing to admit to and compensate for their past mistakes. Historically, such individuals have not tended to do so, nor likely will they ever. Policymakers can easily compound prior errors in judgment. They can also lay the groundwork for an aggressive inflationary psychology to take hold and spin wildly out of control, especially if circumstances are just right

That can happen easily when a devastated economy, massive government debt, empirical overstretch, unparalleled financial imbalances, an unwillingness to cut spending or raise taxes, and an unstable geopolitical framework forces policymakers to abandon prudence in favor of creating a lot more money out of thin air. But loss of faith in a currency is not only a manifestation of bad monetary policy; it can also reflect changing attitudes about the country in question.

In the case of the United States, foreigners were already becoming less accommodating by 2006, a perspective no doubt exacerbated by the nearly $1 trillion cost of the war in Iraq. Polls also confirmed that there had been widespread acceptance out-side the United States of a shifting world order. That vulnerability extended to discussions about America's creditworthiness, which was once viewed as an unrivaled standard of excellence. In June 2006, Standard & Poor's rating service noted: "Without concert-ed policy and fiscal reforms, the aging population would lead to intense pressure on the public finances and the ratings" of the United States. In fact, S&P suggested that by 2025, the U.S. sover-eign credit rating could end up in the "junk" category if present circumstances continued.

Adding to the precariousness of the situation was the fact that the world was awash in dollars, with around two-thirds of global reserves held in American currency, according to International Monetary Fund data. The once unrivaled superpower had be-come dangerously reliant on the largesse of foreigners, who had been almost inexplicably willing to finance years of compulsive spending and borrowing. Under the circumstances, a crisis of con-fidence was the last thing the United States needed. Nonetheless, when the Federal Reserve Board and other policymakers eventu-ally succumb to the realities of a nation crushed under the weight of gargantuan government debt, a financial system in crisis, and a crippling economic depression, they will have little choice but to follow the Zimbabweans.

At first, the Fed may put into effect the policies implemented by Japan after 2000 in response to its own deflationary economic woes: zero interest rates and "quantitative easing," gorging the banking system with reserves. But over time, following a growing unwillingness by American individuals and businesses to borrow for either consumption or investment, the Fed will likely adopt an even more aggressive stance and rely upon what are euphemisti-cally referred to as "unconventional" methods.

In other words, they will "monetize" anything that moves.

Instead of buying only fixed-income securities in the open market, the Fed may very well expand its horizons to include stocks, gold, real estate, banks, businesses, or perhaps used automobiles—whatever it takes to turn the situation around. They may even follow the hypothetical suggestion once made by Fed chair Ben Bernanke and literally drop currency out of helicopters. Although such a move will may provide a temporary respite, it will also serve to vastly expand the money supply, helping to accelerate an already full-fledged collapse in the dollar.

Politicians and policymakers will argue publicly that domestic concerns are far more important than foreign currency markets, while overseas holders head for the hills. Many will have already come around to Warren Buffett's notion, as earlier reported in the *Wall Street Journal,* that "[t]he more you owe, the more it becomes attractive to devalue the currency in which the nation's debts are denominated."

But not only foreigners will be selling. More than likely, crashing markets and an increasingly widespread loss of faith in Washington's ability to stem a rising red tide will also spur significant capital flight. Those with the wherewithal to do so will open accounts and secure safe-deposit boxes in certain tax havens and traditionally "safe" locales; transfer funds; buy easily transportable stores of value such as gold, silver, and diamonds; and invest in foreign real estate and other assets held outside our shores.

Unfortunately, with unemployment rising sharply and domestic house prices still playing out the tail end of a seemingly slow-motion and never-ending freefall, the vast majority of Americans won't have that luxury. Most will struggle even more than they did during the first phase of the unraveling just to make ends meet amid widespread downsizing, limited or no access to credit, and cutbacks in public assistance and a wide range of vital services.

At first, consumers under siege will be forced to ration household spending and take a variety of economizing steps, as higher prices for imported goods and the fallout from a surging money supply eat away at their purchasing power. Over time, the crisis of confidence in currency and other markets, as well as continuing reports of widespread price increases, will trigger a dramatic mind-set reversal, despite government efforts to disguise bad news with distorted data and obfuscation. People will realize that by holding back on purchases, they lose out, because with each day that passes, they can afford less and less. By then, Americans will try to spend whatever they have as fast as they can, and the shift into inflationary overdrive will begin in earnest.

Hyperinflation represents an Alice-in-Wonderland extreme with which few people can come to grips. What most people perceive as prudence during normal economic times can be disastrous when prices are going through the roof. It makes sense, for instance, to keep as little money as possible in a bank account and to convert whatever is on hand into basic necessities, assets, or commodities that will hold their value—or even exchange cash for other, more stable currencies—as quickly as possible.

One of the hallmarks of a period of rapidly rising prices is the redistribution of wealth and the clear-cut distinctions that emerge between winners and losers. Unlike during a depression, borrowers can benefit at the expense of lenders, especially with regard to fixed-payment debts they incurred beforehand. The public sector also tends to gain an advantage compared to the population at large, even relative to those who don't pay taxes. In essence, modest inflation is a tax, whereas hyperinflation more closely resembles a form of wealth confiscation.

Regardless, public services usually decline under such conditions, while infrastructure is allowed to fall into a dangerous state of disrepair. That is because much of the money flowing through government coffers is squandered or spent to maintain the standard of living of the public employees who support the status quo. During a period of hyperinflation, normal perspectives about finance and time horizons don't apply to earning a living, spending, borrowing, or investing. In Weimar Germany, for example, prices effectively doubled every 49 hours at the peak of the spiral in 1923. By then, according to a December 1999 report in the *Economist*, workers were paid twice a day and were given "half-hour breaks to rush to the shops with their satchels, suitcases, or wheelbarrow to buy something, anything, before their paper money halved in value again."

Where inflation soars, the urge to convert cash into something else almost resembles a game of "hot potato." When those who have it don't spend it on immediate needs, they automatically exchange it for something else. Hoarding tangible assets, which might include precious metals, jewelry, antiques, works of art, and land, is common. Moreover, despite many shortcomings, bartering is a popular strategy when the domestic currency is under assault. Historically, it has not been uncommon for at least some workers to prefer being paid in hard goods, such as farm products, which tend to hold their value and can be exchanged for other items.

Bank runs have also been a recurring feature during past hyperinflationary episodes, as depositors queue up to withdraw their savings and spend the cash before price rises wipe out whatever they had saved or invested. In fact, in the treacherous times ahead, Americans will also have to worry increasingly about not having access to their money at all, as failures multiply and fears grow over which financial institutions will be the next to slam shut their doors.

In a situation where inflation is spiraling rapidly out of control, the cost and technical nuances of credit—if it is even available—can also become distorted, and once again the normal rules won't apply. Using credit cards, if allowed at all, will cause confusion and misrepresentation about rates, due dates, and charges. Many vendors will refuse to accept them, while others will adjust prices to account for even the smallest of delays they face in getting reimbursed.

All of these deviations from the norm will compound the problems of an already crumbling economy, making decisions about production and investment even more difficult. As a result, an ever-widening range of businesses will be forced to cut staff to the bone or shut down completely. During past hyperinflation periods, some domestic manufacturing firms that remained in business stopped producing goods altogether and became actively involved in speculation, profiteering, and pricing arbitrage. Many manufacturers will generate more returns that way than through traditional efforts.

The combination of pricing distortions, business shutdowns, and misallocated resources invariably leads to blackouts and shortages, especially of low-margin, commodity-type products. Many basic necessities will become luxuries virtually impossible to find at legitimate retailers. In some instances, parallel or black markets will fill the gaps with goods brought in through dubious channels or simply stolen domestically.

Surging unemployment is a common feature of hyperinflation. More than likely, the U.S. jobless rate will rise far above the extraordinary levels last seen during the Great Depression, when one in four Americans was out of work. For those that manage to find or keep a job, real earnings growth will almost certainly lag behind price increases for most goods and services, leaving people increasingly worse off. Wages are not often adjusted upward as fast as are retail prices, while marginal tax rates tend not to be fully indexed to a rapidly changing inflation rate. Lower pay scales overseas will also cap what U.S. employers are willing to pay.

Poverty, homelessness, and hunger, already much in evidence by the time hyperinflation kicks in, will worsen considerably, adding to a general mood of despair and helplessness. Over time, widespread want will spur increasing unrest, leading to almost continuous strikes, protests, and violence. In some cases, individuals will band together in ad hoc gangs or organized groups for self-protection. Workers of all stripes will do the same, and union membership will rebound sharply after falling for decades. Evidence suggests that collective bargainers tend to be strongest when people feel almost bereft of economic power, as has long been the case in many Latin American nations.

The urge to lay blame and to identify scapegoats will likely become even more pronounced as people grow steadily angrier and more confused about what is happening. No doubt those targeted will include the usual suspects: business leaders, bankers, speculators, and foreigners.

If history repeats itself, policymakers and politicians will be forced to try to end the madness, especially when inflation begins a surrealistic, rapidly self-sustaining spiral. As has often been the case in other countries that faced a similar disaster, most early efforts will take little or no account of basic economic realities and will focus instead on ineffective quick fixes such as propaganda and wage and price controls. Depending on how bad things become, the government will likely take more aggressive steps, including limiting withdrawals or electronic debits; implementing mandatory conversions of foreign currency savings and securities holdings into dollar equivalents; curtailing foreign exchange activities; and confiscating private holdings of gold, silver, and other tangible goods. In the worst case, the United States may default on, or effectively repudiate, some or all of its obligations.

By this point, domestic and international tensions will have reached a fever pitch, and global commerce will be in a tailspin. Talk of trade wars and sharply rising tariffs will surface everywhere, and many nations will respond to the dollar's weakness by engaging in competitive "beggar thy neighbor" devaluations of their own. Severe shortages of basic necessities, double-digit unemployment, and festering social tensions will spur revolutionary movements in places like the Mideast, Asia, and Latin America. In the United States and elsewhere, the government will try to limit civil liberties; restrict the flow of money, trade, and ideas internally and across borders; and even impose full-fledged martial law.

After many years of crisis and despair, it will seem as though the world has well and truly come to an end.

FALLOUT

9

ECONOMIC

*"The worst is not
so long as we can say, 'This is the worst.'"*

—William Shakespeare

The storyline of the 1999 film *Double Jeopardy* goes something like this: A woman imprisoned for the murder of her missing husband later discovers that she was set up as part of a $2 million insurance scam by her sleazy spouse, who is still very much alive. Angered by the deceit, she vows to exact revenge by rubbing him out for real when she is released from jail, believing that she cannot be brought to justice because of a constitutional ban against being tried more than once for the same crime.

Although the premise of the film leaves something to be desired—killing her husband, even if he was already thought to be dead, would still be a wholly separate and punishable offence—the protections enshrined in the Fifth Amendment are hallmarks of the American legal system. Nonetheless, safeguards afforded to defendants in criminal trials don't necessarily extend to other circumstances. Acquitted wrongdoers can be penalized, albeit only monetarily, if they are deemed at fault in a civil trial. Supreme Court opinions have held that people who violate the laws of more than one jurisdiction can be held doubly accountable and tried accordingly. Typically, though, these exceptions have applied only to a relatively small number of individuals.

But when it comes to the financial penalties that accrue from decades of ill-conceived, irresponsible, or corrupt policies, few safeguards will prevent millions of people from being repeatedly whipped by economic misfortune. In all likelihood, the depression-cum-hyperinflation disaster ahead will be a case of economic double jeopardy from which the foolish or unwary have little escape. When it happens, people will become acutely aware of the ethereal nature of the American dream.

From earning a living and sustaining a certain lifestyle; to borrowing, investing, and spending money; to the adequacy and availability of social, financial, and other safety nets, much of what we have taken for granted will be called into question. But what will make matters far worse is that the overall process will be long and drawn out. Many of those who believe they've somehow survived will, in one way or another, face a rude awakening.

During the first phase, those who owe a lot of money and don't have much in terms of savings or other resources, or who are one of the more than 37 million Americans already living below the poverty line, will bear the full weight of suffering and impoverishment. But soon those in the next segment up, the 54 million vulnerable individuals, who, according to the *New York Times*, are in "households earning between the poverty line and double the poverty line," will also be submerged by the economic tsunami.

As malaise turns into full-blown depression, hiring will slow to a near standstill, and even the toughest and most unappealing jobs will be hard to find. Yet rising unemployment won't just be the result of business uncertainty and falling demand. Adding to the pressure on labor markets, as the *Wall Street Journal* has pointed out, will be 1.5 billion workers from China, India, and the former Soviet Union who will join the ranks of the global labor force as those countries become capitalist economies.

Domestic influences will be at work too. Lacking adequate nest eggs and pensions, some of those who might have once considered retiring at age 65 will have no choice but to remain in the workforce until the day they die. They will discover, usually too late, that the promises they were depending on for their golden years are unavailable because of bankruptcies or opportunism, incompetence, or gross negligence. Other obligations that were once an integral part of the compact between employers and employees will be readily cast aside. That move will be easy enough to justify when corporate survival options are limited.

In a rapidly burgeoning job seeker's market, older Americans will be joined by legions of formerly nonworking spouses and teenage children who will have been pressured to seek out extra sources of income to help their families make ends meet. But even those with financial cushions at the beginning of the great unraveling can't be sure that the one-two punch of depression and runaway inflation won't still shear them clean. In fact, people who were astute or lucky enough to accumulate wealth might not be better off. Unless they have mainly invested in cash, many of those with stocks, bonds, and other property, especially if financed with debt, will see their net worth take a substantial hit during the first phase. In many cases, they will effectively have nothing at all. Asset prices will be enmeshed in a relentless, often violent downward spiral, exacerbated by selling from overextended debtors, foolhardy speculators, and other casualties of the credit-inspired boom as they suffer the consequences of years of short-sighted exuberance.

The onset of a long cycle of demographic-induced selling pressure, as aging Americans naturally seek safer havens for whatever savings or investments they have remaining, will also weigh on markets. So will a persistent and broadening shift away from risk toward safety. The combination of forced liquidations, asset reallocations, and a constant fear of losing money will feed a vicious cycle of selling that begets further selling, putting the final nail into the coffin of gratuitous bubble building. After repeated waves of home equity borrowing, mortgage refinancing, and debt rollovers, many Americans will decide that it is better to hand over the keys to the house, vacation retreat, and cars than to be enslaved to the interests of lenders for years to come.

Regardless, those at the low end of the economic ladder will doubtless be hurt the most, and the gulf between poor and rich—or even, perhaps, the not-so-rich—will widen even more than it has in recent decades. Already stagnating in inflation-adjusted terms when conditions were allegedly in a permanent plateau-like state, wages will increasingly lag behind other economic measures when the situation really turns ugly. At first, many overstretched consumers will attempt to maintain the trappings of a life spent keeping up with the Joneses. If the Great Depression is any guide, those who are exposed will initially seek out short-term financing. Or they may very well deny themselves such basic necessities as food or clothing to hang on to prized, debt-financed possessions such as homes and cars.

Others will have to make the most difficult choices: Should they go food shopping or pay the electric bill? Should they replace worn-out shoes or top up the tank with gasoline so they can get to work? Should they pay for a babysitter to look after the children when they come home from school or skip their breakfast and lunch that day? Whatever the case, Americans will reduce spending at virtually every level, either because they don't have the money or because they fear losing what they have. During sustained hard times, formerly wanton consumers will attempt to do what they've avoided for years: save for a rainy day.

No doubt businesses that can afford it will try to counter that trend by offering ever more generous deals and incentives. These might include seemingly suicidal rebates, sizable discounts for cash, superextended warranties, all kinds of "free" extras, and—even in a world where debt is becoming anathema—an array of long-term and special-rate financing options. Some may even resort to desperate measures, like offering risky customers the option of having electronic devices attached to automobiles, appliances, and other products that allow them to function only if debt payments are up-to-date.

But with Americans transformed from indulgent squanderers into consumer zombies, those efforts will prove costly and the effects short-lived. One consequence: A nation of malls will witness thousands of retailers shutting their doors—in many cases forever. Businesses on the front line of consumer-related spending won't be the only ones to feel the ripple effect of declining economic activity. Many industrial goods makers and service-related concerns, together with banks and other financial intermediaries, will be driven into bankruptcy. Those firms that manage to stay afloat will have to engage in ruthless cost cutting and make do with less in terms of margins and revenues—and employees.

As the debacle evolves from economic contraction to runaway inflation, a new stage of wealth destruction and impoverishment will begin. For the most part, phase two of the crisis will target creditors and the wealthy as well as those who managed, in one way or another, to put something aside when they had the opportunity. The fallout from hyperinflation will be dramatic and widespread, with the remains of whatever cash, business operations, and financial assets that were salvaged from the earlier wreckage suddenly in peril.

During hyperinflation, millionaires who can't afford to buy anything are literally a dime a dozen. It won't take long, in fact, for those with any measure of financial wherewithal to realize that if they don't immediately change their behavior, they will experience a devastating loss of purchasing power. Eventually, everyone will be in a mad dash to get rid of their cash before prices surge further. In the wake of dramatically changing attitudes and circumstances, uncertainty and upheaval will quickly follow.

Companies that had come to rely on ready access to credit, just-in-time purchasing and inventory management, streamlined logistics, or efficient global trading networks will discover that their business models are totally unsuited to a world of compounding inefficiencies, social chaos, and random economic dislocations. In some cases, the owners and overseers of firms that remain open will become dangerously distracted or devote much of their time and energy to speculative pursuits such as commodities trading and arbitrage. Whether they are buying or selling, others will struggle to keep afloat in an environment where pricing is extraordinarily fluid and nonlinear.

The mishmash of unfamiliar operating patterns and bizarre distortions will strain an already growing disparity between what the marketplace needs and what is available, leading to continual and widespread shortages as well as a great deal of waste. Rationing, whether compulsory or instituted on an ad hoc basis, will be commonplace, especially of oil and other forms of imported energy. And because agriculture in particular depends heavily on petrochemical products, constrained supplies will likely have a substantial impact on the availability and price of a wide variety of foodstuffs.

Throughout history, rapidly rising prices have fostered a near universal reluctance to hold monetary assets for any length of time. As the hyperinflation becomes full-blown, Americans with cash at their disposal will see things the same way. They will look to spend their money as quickly as possible, either by shopping for essentials or by investing it in something that they hope will retain some measure of its value. Their behavior will further exacerbate imbalances between supply and demand and spur increased hoarding of food and other necessities as well as a variety of tangible assets. Increasingly, warehouses will be piled to the ceiling with goods held off the market in anticipation of still-higher prices, adding further fuel to the raging inflationary fire. Not coincidently, dire conditions will also stimulate a preference for barter transactions and a flourishing underground economy free of taxes, red tape, and other government interference.

After unsuccessfully trying to solve problems that they played a starring role in creating, Washington and state and local governments will inevitably attempt to rectify matters with disastrous "solutions" that further defy the laws of economics. From underreporting, distorting, or hiding inflation and money supply statistics, to implementing wage and price controls, to limiting access to one's own funds, lawmakers and government agencies will try every trick in the book—except to decrease the supply of worthless currency—to turn things around. But the measures will prove as fruitless as those introduced in the early 1970s. Then, the Nixon administration implemented economy-wide wage and price controls that lasted for two years to stem apparent rampant inflation. Those rules eventually led to shortages of beef, metals, building materials, and even toilet seats, which forced some construction projects to temporarily shut down.

In such an environment, people on fixed incomes or pensions will discover that they are easy targets for official action. Whatever isn't taken away from them by hyperinflation will likely be confiscated at least partly through other means. One approach might be the introduction of caps on cost-of-living adjustments or the mandatory conversion of retirement savings balances into dollar-denominated, long-term government debt. Or lawmakers will impose restrictions similar to those that certain Latin American nations have adopted, whereby depositors seeking access to funds held at banks and other financial institutions are limited in terms of how much and how often they can withdraw.

These efforts will do little to stem the flow of greenbacks to other currencies; basic necessities; or hard goods such as precious metals, commodities, and even real estate. The timing may be opportune, as many of these assets will likely have declined in value to multidecade lows during the prior liquidation phase. Ironically, even in the face of a hyperinflation-fed turnaround in nominal asset prices, more and more homeowners will not benefit, because they will be weighed down by myriad financial woes, including variable- or fixed-rate mortgages taken on during the boom times. Foreclosure will loom as the relentless decline in real personal income takes its toll.

Owning rapidly expanding inventories of seized property might not be an advantage for lenders when they are besieged by a suffocating array of financial, legal, and operational troubles of their own. Some may even adopt an air of pseudo-benevolence and bend over backward to stem the surge of foreclosures and the resulting political pressures. Others will, out of desperation, welcome the kind of runaway inflation that bankers have long feared in the hope that they will themselves be rescued from the debt-filled abyss.

With many traditional avenues shut, individuals who are out of work will invariably go knocking on doors, looking for loans and handouts from family and friends. No small number will turn to loan sharks and other vultures that thrive in times of trouble. The overall quality of life will likely be a far cry from that of the late 20th century. Attitudes and relationships will sour. The mood will turn gloomy amid a widespread deterioration in day-to-day living conditions. In a world of potholed roads and broken windows, polluted beaches and empty houses with overgrown lawns, people begging and crying on corner after corner, and of hordes of newly homeless adults and children, sentiment will succumb to the negative.

This will be especially true when the backstop that Americans assumed would be there is no longer available, because the combined bullets of a social safety net, expansive fiscal policy, and an aggressive monetary stimulus have already been spent. By then, in fact, a growing array of public assistance programs and vital government services will be fading from view or fail miserably as a result of aggressive budget cutting necessitated by falling tax revenues or lenders turning off the tap.

In some regions, already overcrowded schools will shorten the number of hours in a day or the length of a term, while publicly funded day care centers, drop-in medical clinics, and other lifelines for the poor and downtrodden will disappear. Numerous public and private colleges and universities will be forced to close, as funding is cut and prospective students abandon plans for advanced study because of family financial problems. During such times, the need to bring home the bacon will matter more than an enlightened mind.

Crime will run rampant as police departments and other government services that help maintain public order eliminate or cut back on jobs, overtime, and equipment, while growing numbers of formerly law-abiding but now desperate citizens reveal their dark side. In place of welfare and other taxpayer-funded assistance programs, suffering families will have little choice but to turn to a shrinking universe of overburdened charities and informal support networks, such as "backpack clubs," where children fill up empty packs on Fridays with donated food so they will have something to eat over the weekend.

During the early 1930s, families were forced to split up or move elsewhere in search of employment. Some ended up in shantytowns, known as "Hoovervilles" after Herbert Hoover, who was president when the Great Depression began. They lived in squalor in rickety shelters made of crates, old cars, and other cast-offs. In the wake of the early 21st-century housing boom, the migratory landing points may well be the millions of condominiums and boarded-up new homes left empty or mired in foreclosure in what were once the hottest real estate markets.

Although such accommodation might represent an improvement over life during the Great Depression, the angst and suffering will be the same. Odds are that many of those who have been cut loose won't eat properly or be able to afford adequate health care, leading to an array of debilitating ailments. Deteriorating health, sanitation, and pest control will lay the groundwork for tuberculosis and other epidemics, as well as virulent pandemics like SARS. These diseases will not only endanger the lives of millions but will also create a sense of isolation and uncertainty that will add to the downward spiral.

Feeling trapped and desperate, countless ordinary Americans will be wracked with feelings of bitterness, resentment, guilt, and frustration as they find it hard to come to grips with the pervasive fallout of a full-scale economic disaster. Over time, those feelings are likely to boil over in rage with disturbing frequency. Increasingly, an evolving sense that people have nothing to lose will turn feelings of shame and hopelessness into a desire for revenge.

News of strikes over pay and poor working conditions, endlessly long lines, marches over rising taxes or unemployment, and riots over food and fuel prices or access to social services will be commonplace. As protests become more frequent, many others will be emboldened to join in, making matters worse. No matter where you look, fear and uncertainty will be in the air.

10

FINANCIAL

*"Finance is the art of passing money from
hand to hand until it finally disappears."*
—Robert W. Sarnoff

In his 1994 book *Target Risk,*
Dr. Gerald Wilde discusses a theory known as "risk homeostasis,"
which holds that human beings strive to maintain a more or less
constant level of exposure to perceived risk. As an example, he
cites a study commissioned by the German transport ministry,
which monitored the pattern of accidents incurred by drivers for
a Munich-based taxicab company in the midst of changing over to
vehicles with antilock braking systems (ABS).

In theory, the move to ABS-equipped cars should have led to
fewer fender benders and wipeouts. In reality, drivers with the newer brakes showed little improvement in their accident rate and actually had more mishaps when conditions were slippery than did
the drivers of vehicles with standard braking systems. The reason
was that those who drove the "safer" cars changed their behavior.
Among other things, they "made sharper turns in curves, were
less accurate in their lane-holding" behavior, and "proceeded at a
shorter forward sight distance" than did their colleagues, according to the study.

In many respects, the nature of modern finance, with its labyrinth of rules, regulatory regimes, risk management tools, high-powered computers, and accoutrements of sophisticated analysis has provoked a similar response. Rather than making the financial infrastructure stable and resilient, the latticework of apparent safety measures seems to have encouraged fearlessness and recklessness, especially where people have plenty of incentives to roll the dice and go for broke. As a result, banks, brokers, and other financial operators have engaged in ever riskier behavior. This enhanced appetite for risk has made the financial system far more vulnerable to catastrophic meltdown than many believed possible.

Other seemingly beneficial developments have also had unexpected consequences. William Gross, managing director of PIMCO, noted in 2005: "Although financial innovation and derivative products allow for diversification and a spreading of risk across more market players, the increased liquidity has . . . allowed for increased leverage, quicker exits, and therefore more systemic, systemwide risk." Virtually all financial systems are pyramid-like structures built on a tenuous foundation of faith and trust. Moreover, they depend on a great many often untested assumptions for their continued existence and smooth functioning. But when enough of those supporting planks disappear, the consequences can be devastating. Throughout history, financial crises and banking panics have frequently been the precursors of recessions and depressions and, occasionally, full-scale economic collapses.

Six years after the equity bubble burst in the spring of 2000, there were numerous signs that a systemic destabilization was nearly underway. And with that, much of what had been taken for granted in an era of homes-as-ATMs, derivatives, securitization, and other forms of modern financial alchemy would suddenly be called into question. Until that point, people assumed that liquidity in all forms would remain more or less the same, despite a 180-degree turnaround in global monetary conditions and an increasingly hostile market environment. The idea of not having access to one's own funds was almost inconceivable.

People had made a similar collective assumption about the nature of all sorts of financial relationships, from those that linked counterparties and constituents of the modern financial system to those among securities, products, and markets, and those that bound together nations and economic regions. Many people believed that the business cycle, or at least the downward-sloping half of it, was a relic of the past, and that the dramatic financial crises that had unsettled the landscape as recently as 1998 were no longer a factor, especially with the Fed and other regulators standing at the ready.

All of that was about to change, however, as an economic and financial house of cards built on debt, delusion, distortion, and excess began to tumble. Phenomena that were previously linked will become independent, while markets that were formerly uncorrelated will move in tandem. Historical patterns that served as the cornerstones of strategies driving trillion-dollar investment decisions will increasingly prove worthless.

So too will Americans' belief in one another's rationality and integrity as well as the confidence that bankers, investors, and regulators had acted with an inherent sense of responsibility. Many might have once assumed that even if there were a few bad apples, there were not enough to spoil the entire pie. Yet as the economic and financial tide turns, transforming a sea of apparent calm into a waterfall of fear and insecurity, much of what Americans took for granted will turn out to have been wrong.

People will see just how fleeting liquidity really is, especially when those who have taken on too much of the same risk, who use comparable models and methods to manage it, and who react in like fashion to analogous structural, organizational, and emotional pressures, head for the exits at the same time. For all its benefits, securitization will turn out to be a double-edged sword. Instead of dispersing risk, the process will have served to poison financial waters around the globe. It will be apparent that many banks that had repackaged and supposedly off-loaded mortgages and other obligations as asset-backed securities had actually retained the riskiest pieces for themselves, either out of greed or under pressure from end-investors to keep a bit of "skin" in the game.

Allegedly savvy operators will be found to have turned their attention to all kinds of less-than-beneficial activities, including indulging in rampant speculation, running huge portfolios of suddenly unmanageable derivative positions, and lending money to the least creditworthy borrowers they could find. Hedge funds caught wrong-footed when the music stops, or investors with limited knowledge of the risks involved—including many municipal governments, insurers, and smaller banks—will turn out to have been the dumping ground for much toxic financial waste.

With their rose-colored glasses off, people will see—again, belatedly—that although risk had theoretically been dispersed, it has actually puddled clandestinely around a small number of operators. These include the largest financial institutions in the country, some of which play a critical role in the nation's settlement and payment infrastructure. No doubt Americans will realize that with so many different types of risk sliced, diced, mixed, matched, and redistributed, the financial landscape is becoming polluted until unrecognizable and unmanageable, especially as conditions deteriorate. In other words, what might once have been a case of plain-vanilla credit risk was now a lethal concoction of credit, interest rate, prepayment, counterparty, and operational risk.

The massive buildup of the securitization machine that began in earnest during the 1990s and reached a crescendo during the mortgage-lending and refinancing boom of the early 21st century will have other harmful side effects. Aside from enabling an orgy of credit creation—whether explicitly agreed to or not by policymakers remains an open question—the process of recycling home, auto, credit card, and other loans into bundles and passing them off means that lenders have few incentives to keep tabs on borrowers. Rather, it is in their interests to lend money to anybody who asks. Because the 1990s included an unusually long span without a severe economic downturn, it should be no surprise when individuals and companies default in droves as conditions worsen.

Instead of eliminating what was essentially a cyclical problem, securitization has created an overflowing mess that will contaminate the financial groundwater for years to come.

The process of converting illiquid obligations and risks into marketable securities played a supporting role in the transformation of the financial services industry and will help exacerbate the damage caused by plunging markets. Along with the sharp increase in global trade, which opened channels through which all sorts of economic shocks could be readily transmitted, the links between financial services providers and the real economy ensure that pressures will now spread quickly. Many of the largest and most heavily leveraged global operators, for example, are subject to margin requirements that are based on their exposure to a broad range of markets, so difficulties in any one area invariably create a ripple effect. They also rely on an active portfolio approach to managing risk, guaranteeing that small or localized problems quickly turn contagious.

Amid the unfolding catastrophe, Americans will become acutely aware of the astonishing degree of leverage that has permeated both Main Street and Wall Street, with much of the borrowed money used for consumption and speculation rather than productive investment. They will be confronted, too, by the reality that massive borrowing was funded for the most part by lenders unwilling (in the case of many foreign creditors) or unable (in the case of banks feeling a great deal of financial pressure themselves) to do so forever. As the credit cycle makes an abrupt about-face, stock, bond, currency, and commodity markets will immediately feel the impact. No doubt the reverberations will be especially pronounced when an abrupt cutting off of financing triggers cascades of forced liquidations. Together with the fallout from a deflating real estate bubble, deteriorating credit conditions will lead to substantial casualties.

But not only individuals, firms, and public-sector authorities are exposed. The victims will also include government-sponsored enterprises (GSEs), banks, and insurers that have pledged to stand behind trillions of dollars of asset-backed securities, municipal bonds, and various obligations. This includes Fannie Mae and Freddie Mac, which will suffer under waves of defaults by overextended homeowners. Hundreds of thousands, or perhaps millions, of mortgagees will be reeling in the aftermath of double-digit percentage increases in their adjustable-rate loan payments.

Diminishing credit ratings will exert downward pressure on the prices of securities that the two mortgage behemoths have guaranteed or issued, including the more than $1 trillion of own-brand mortgage-backed securities (MBSs) they bought using borrowed money. That will, in turn, spur even more downgrades, driving prices still lower. With interest rates also fluctuating wildly on the heels of collapsing markets, heightened systemic fears, and a crumbling economy, one or both of the GSEs will discover that the "perfect storm" insolvency scenario envisaged by Emil Henry, assistant U.S. Treasury secretary, in 2006 had come to fruition, pushing an already teetering property market over the edge.

In an almost entirely market-driven financial arena, a series of shock waves will likely emanate from similarly constructed negative feedback loops. Chaotic conditions and persistent credit downgrades will spur jolts that lead to more of the same. But the daisy-chain disaster won't necessarily end there. Gut-wrenching volatility and failing firms will also play havoc with business and consumer sentiment. That will further ratchet up the rate of belt tightening and liquidations, eventually circling around in a kind of economic pincer movement.

Large-scale bets on the creditworthiness of major industrial and financial concerns will wreak havoc throughout the financial system. Under the circumstances, the advantages of size and a broad exposure to a range of financial activities could turn out to be little more than a cruel joke, tempered only slightly by the increasingly tenuous assumption that certain institutions cannot be allowed to fail without risking economic anarchy. In the private equity sector, where banks and other operators with far more money than sense boosted the financing of illiquid assets and economically sensitive businesses to unbelievable extremes, the failures and fund meltdowns will occur at a quickening pace.

Even taking all of that into account, what will really throw everyone off is the rapidity with which markets seize up, financial institutions shut their doors, and the overall unwinding process progresses. Some past crises have materialized in virtually no time at all. Historically, the pace of decline has been influenced by factors such as how much leverage exists, the fragility of balance sheets, economic and monetary conditions, and the presence of illegal activity or serious mismanagement. When they all line up in one direction, the situation can easily take an abrupt turn for the worse.

In *Bailout: An Insider's Account of Bank Failures and Rescues*, Irvine Sprague notes that "[o]n occasion, the failure of a bank comes with lightning speed. In cases of fraud or runs, the failure can be dramatically fast." Continental Illinois, a bank that went belly-up in 1984, "succumbed in days," according to the former industry insider, because of overly aggressive lending practices and a dependence on short-term borrowing and large, uninsured deposits to meet its funding needs.

Odds are that the often-cited benefits of faster communications, high-powered computers, real-time portfolio pricing, and an aggressive approach to investing won't be seen in the same light when many people are hitting the panic buttons at once. Adding to the misery will be the recognition that many allegedly sophisticated investors had struck something of a Faustian bargain during the good times, by either exchanging immense quantities of borrowed money for unsalable assets or hedging nonmarketable investments with liquid securities. They will be in no position to cut and run, even if they figure out what is happening from the start.

Those counting on regulatory authorities to bail them out will also face a rude awakening. For one thing, the compounding firestorm of a collapsing economy, plunging markets, widespread business failures, geopolitical explosions, and social upheaval will almost certainly lead either to disproportionate overreactions or bureaucratic paralysis. After the Fed is blamed for needlessly choking the economy to death and opening the floodgates to a hyperinflationary spiral, while simultaneously being accused of not doing anywhere near enough, the central bank may find its own days are numbered just like its predecessors, the First Bank and the Second Bank of the United States, which both ceased to exist at the end of their 20-year charters.

Amid widespread political impotence and regulatory incompetence, the prospect of a disappearing Fed will only add to a far-reaching crisis of confidence. Growing numbers of Americans will worry profusely about how they will cope and whether their dwindling resources will be accessible. As economic, financial, and political pressures build, so too will feelings of frustration, anger, anxiety, and betrayal. This will feed an expansive search to uncover the truth and an aggressive hunt to track down those who are in any way responsible.

Meanwhile, newfound transparency in the wake of the unfolding financial crisis will expose a scale of fraud, corruption, and self-dealing that many will find almost impossible to comprehend. Day in and day out, reports will surface about hidden losses, false accounting, inflated appraisals, sizable off-balance-sheet obligations, valuation discrepancies, unregulated offshore entities, phantom profits, insider trading, and businesses bled dry to enrich a few individuals at the expense of employees, investors, bankers, and bondholders. Other revelations will reinforce the idea that companies, governments, and individuals are in far worse shape than people had assumed only a few years earlier. Much like the child watching the royal parade in Hans Christian Anderson's tale "The Emperor's New Clothes," they will be bewildered by the starkness of businesses lacking any real substance.

Numerous banks and financial institutions will be revealed as having been thoroughly mismanaged and looted to an astonishing degree. Many others will remain barely afloat amid the fallout from an unwinding credit bubble and decades of excess, as hordes of struggling debtors stop making payments or simply hand over what they "owned." Over time, thousands of financial intermediaries, including the overextended lending arms of automakers and other industrial concerns, will be forced to shut their doors, adding to spiraling unemployment and growing market turmoil.

As insured losses multiply and eat away at whatever remains of banks' diminishing capital, payoffs will begin to slow down, and Washington will likely take at least some steps to water down or even abolish the FDIC guarantee. Reports and rumors of bad loans, shady deals, and imprudent investments will sap already waning confidence. Panicky account holders will repeatedly rush into banking halls and brokerage offices around the country, anxiously trying to get their money out while they can. Unfortunately, even before the meltdown reaches the terminal stage, many people will discover that they are out of luck. Whatever hadn't been destroyed by inflation or tied up in bankruptcy or other proceedings will probably be rendered at least partly inaccessible because of government decrees, banking "holidays," or liquidity pressures.

Ultimately, bank, money market, mutual fund, and other accounts will likely be frozen or see harsh limits imposed on the amounts that can be withdrawn. In some cases, holders will be forced to accept government IOUs in lieu of cash. Debit and credit card usage may also be sharply curtailed, triggering massive shock waves and chaos in an age when people have become almost completely dependent on electronic transactions. The effective losses to account holders at financial institutions, as well as unexpectedly uninsured depositors at banks around the country, are likely to far exceed the 19 percent seen during the Great Depression.

But those individuals won't be the only ones to see their economic well-being and longer-term prospects plunging into a sinkhole. Those who spent a lifetime saving and scrimping or who were promised a fixed or even an inflation-linked payout after disability or retirement will be under constant threat as well. Even the wealthy—perhaps "formerly wealthy" would be more accurate—won't escape unscathed. Unless they have moved their assets to safer locales and nimbly played each phase of the disaster, they will find themselves caught in the crossfire of economic and financial Armageddon.

With their exposure to falling asset prices and a rapidly depreciating currency, foreign holders of American assets will fare especially poorly. Their losses will be further compounded by a disorderly "adjustment" of global imbalances and the actions they themselves take to get out of the mess.

For Americans and others, the financial carnage will seem like an exhausting and never-ending war of attrition.

11

SOCIAL

"Moral codes adjust themselves to environmental conditions."
—**William J. Durant**

Many law enforcement officials and criminologists assert that the broken-window theory, which holds that "disorder invites more disorder," played a key role in an unprecedented drop in crime rates in New York City during the 1990s. In a 1996 *New Yorker* article and later in his 2000 bestseller *The Tipping Point*, Malcolm Gladwell recounts the strategy adopted by the city's police department. That agency took its lead from the Transit Authority's earlier successes, which came from eliminating the kinds of trivial problems like subway fare beating and petty vandalism that might lead to more serious crimes.

Despite the apparent connection, some might wonder whether a safer Big Apple had as much to do with the economic groundswell that swept across the nation at that time as with New York City's zero-tolerance policing policy. Sociologist Steven Box would probably have argued in favor of the former after he outlined a strong link between illegal activity and unemployment, poverty, and heightened competition in his 1977 book *Recession, Crime, and*

Punishment. Based on studies undertaken in the United States and elsewhere, Box concluded that a "deterioration in material circumstances does lead to more crime."

No doubt other relationships and circumstances also can affect the willingness of individuals, whether once law abiding or not, to engage in criminal or deviant behavior. Whatever the case, the coming economic and financial disaster will see a broad and powerful combination of catalysts that can trigger frustration, resentment, anger—and a willingness to do whatever it takes to survive. The social fabric will be torn apart as optimism fades; joblessness soars; economic activity wanes; resources are stretched to the breaking point; and cutbacks in spending on law enforcement, social services, and other safety nets fuel desperation and despair.

Much antisocial behavior will likely stem from an urge to satisfy basic needs, including food, adequate shelter, and health care. But it will also reflect the stress of coping with constant fear and uncertainty. In many cases, smaller households will be forced to take in extended family—adult children, elders, and distant relatives—creating a pressure-cooker environment that will regularly come to a boil. As a result, domestic violence and abuse will become even more pressing concerns than in the past.

The rising economic burden and dour outlook will see marriage and birth rates fall and divorce rates rise. These trends will further limit demand for myriad goods and services and push consumer confidence to record lows. Intense competition for jobs and other resources will prove exceptionally divisive as the unraveling moves into high gear. Among other things, it will exacerbate the widening disparity between rich and poor.

Demographic battle lines will harden as a fast-growing and ever more militant class of older Americans throws its weight around in an attempt to preserve retirement, health care, and other benefits. No doubt they will look to foist more and more of these rapidly multiplying economic burdens onto the traditional working-age population. And as economic circumstances continue to worsen, old and young will increasingly find themselves in stiff competition for a dwindling number of jobs, further aggravating generational conflicts over an expanding array of economic and social concerns.

Unfortunately, individuals who fail to find work or secure the ongoing support of family or friends will discover that the holes in the social safety net have grown inordinately wide. Amid over-stretched budgets, squandered resources, and fierce resistance against rising taxes, federal, state, and local government agencies will be under continuing pressure to dilute or eliminate programs for all but the neediest individuals and families. Private charities, meanwhile, will see donations drop precipitously, as economic strains force those who might once have underwritten their ef-forts to scale back philanthropy. Numerous nonprofit organiza-tions will likely go bankrupt trying to meet increased demands for assistance in anticipation of donations that never arrive.

Unable to cope with the harsh new economic environment, growing numbers of Americans will end up on the streets—con-fused, homeless, and hungry. With that, begging will increase to previously unseen levels. So, too, will a range of other social ills, especially when those who have lost hope seek solace in drugs or alcohol. For a small number of individuals, the decaying social framework will unleash the most savage of instincts, leading to an increase in random acts of barbaric violence and murder.

Even once-model citizens will have little choice but to break the law to take care of themselves or their families. To be sure, many breaches will involve opportunistic acts, such as stealing a laptop computer left alone in public, shoplifting merchandise from a store, or walking out of the supermarket without paying for groceries. Crime, especially against property, will become endemic.

Numerous predators will attempt to take advantage of the situ-ation, focusing on the weak and the distressed. Some will offer unconscionable terms for borrowing money and enforce painful consequences on those who don't pay, while others will offer funds in exchange for whatever services they wish rendered. For some in positions of authority, especially in the public sector, corruption will seem like an easy answer to all their problems. They will seek out bribes, whether in cash or in kind, for favors and influence.

Meanwhile, hardcore miscreants will move quickly to expand their operations and capitalize on the deteriorating social structure. They will be actively involved in loan-sharking, prostitution, narcotics, gambling, identity theft, robbery, and a multitude of other illegal activities. During the Great Depression, the Mafia and various criminal gangs made great strides in terms of organization and influence, though they were aided, of course, by their involvement in circumventing an unpopular prohibition of alcohol. Regardless, the period ahead will almost certainly see a similar development, with ruthless homegrown as well as Asian, Eastern European, and Latin American gangsters, many of whom had already gained a foothold in the United States, dramatically expanding their reach and influence.

Unfortunately, they will likely meet with much less resistance than in the past, because law enforcement agencies around the country will be confronted with the same budgetary pressures affecting all government departments. Most will have little choice but to cut back on overtime, hiring, training, raises, and technology. Under the circumstances, conditions are bound to get a lot more dangerous before they improve. That will be especially true in neighborhoods already considered to be in bad shape as well as in the new ghettos that will likely spring up around tracts of homes and condos abandoned in the wake of the burst housing bubble.

Another obstacle to maintaining order will be the criminal justice system: underfunded, understaffed, and overwhelmed with countless proceedings and trials. No doubt, at least some cases will arise from frauds and other crimes hidden from view during earlier boom times. The civil and criminal courts will also be groaning under the weight of an avalanche of lawsuits and writs, as economic circumstances spur a rash of efforts to walk away from all sorts of obligations, including warranties and insurance policies, as well as contracts written and promises made when times were better.

To overcome a sense of powerlessness, many individuals will seek to gain strength through numbers. As noted previously, after a long period of decline, unions will stage a dramatic comeback. Other organizations, whose mission revolves around a common, often economic, bond, as well as fraternal groups whose members agree to look after each others' interests, will also gain in popularity and influence. Along with the urge to exercise power, brewing frustration and a desire for change will provoke myriad collective actions, including protests, strikes, and marches. There will also be riots and frequent bouts of sometimes sickening violence. Increasingly, efforts that start out peacefully will be hijacked by agitators for their own sinister purposes.

In this environment, the established order will be challenged on a number of fronts. But those looking to the government for answers will likely discover that the leadership cupboard is bare. Politicians will run for cover and policymakers will be paralyzed with fear and uncertainty, caught up in a contagious bureaucratic vacuum. As one crisis after another unfolds in rapid succession, most will likely be met with impotence and indecisiveness, buck passing, and a Pollyannaish refusal to recognize the realities of the situation, at least in the beginning. Calls for strong leadership and an aggressive course of action will come into constant conflict with a steady clamor for handouts, bailouts, extra benefits, and special treatment.

Paradoxically, perhaps, American attitudes toward authority will become increasingly polarized, mirroring a broader societal split. Some people will swear an almost fanatical allegiance to the cause of a strong central authority, urging officials in Washington and around the country to adopt an uncompromising stance. Others, in contrast, will lay the blame for existing circumstances on decades of unworkable or irresponsible policies as well as failed leadership. They will increasingly favor dramatic change and some form of popular revolt. Questions and challenges about which side is more patriotic or in sync with the will of the people will lead to frequent and ugly clashes and standoffs, as both the pro- and anti-government sides respond to divergent emotional forces.

A pattern of partisanship and positional intransigence, which seemed to begin in earnest after the invasion of Iraq, will become even more pronounced when the economy is on the skids. Instead of working together to resolve matters, many Democrats and Republicans will get caught up in laying blame and try to gain at least a short-term advantage at the other's expense. In fact, emboldened by a dramatic reversal of fortunes following years of GOP control in Washington, a resurgent Democrat party may well decide that its overriding goal is to obliterate all signs of its rival's legacy, no matter how destructive that course might be. Some die-hard loyalists will press hard for high-profile investigations, impeachments, and even criminal trials.

Over time, the political arena will become utterly intolerant, obstructionist, and radicalized, with many in power appealing more to the wounded spirits of those who feel victimized or disenfranchised than to those looking to make the best of a bad situation. Unfortunately, the circumstances will also create an environment ripe for the cultivation of despotic and dangerous populists, looking to misuse the collective angst and abuse a desire for strong leadership and dramatic change.

Spurred initially by economic realities, an ugly mood of separatism and exclusionism will almost certainly take hold that emphasizes differences, not similarities. "Us and them" will be far more important than simply "we." As the economic situation deteriorates, it will only make matters worse. In a resource-strapped world, where each interaction increasingly resembles a "zero-sum game," one person's gain will invariably be seen as another's loss. Given that, many Americans will feel compelled to reject virtually anyone who is the least bit different—who might in some Darwinian fashion represent a threat to their own survival.

Bigotry and an almost rabid hatred of other races, cultures, and religions will increasingly permeate all levels of society. Anti-Semitic, anti-Muslim, and anti-Christian sentiments are likely to grow in equal measure. Foreigners, in general, and immigrants, in particular, will prove to be easy targets. In fact, America's long dependence on manufactured goods and money borrowed from abroad will spur considerable resentment toward outsiders, reinforcing a broad sense of xenophobic paranoia and efforts to close the nation's borders both figuratively and literally.

Everywhere and anywhere, those seen as rejecting even a small measure of an America-centric perspective will be labeled undesirables, subversives, and even "enemy combatants," whether or not evidence supports the assertion. In the land where the Statue of Liberty once beckoned to all, many visitors will no longer feel welcome. Those seeking to emigrate to, or temporarily reside in, the United States will receive an even chillier reception.

Not surprisingly, deteriorating circumstances will have an increasingly deleterious effect on employer-worker relations. Managers who engage in business survival tactics that include canceling labor contracts, stripping away benefits, and shifting financial risks to employees won't improve the situation. Companies in serious financial straits—not to mention stakeholders, including the local communities that lose big when area employers fail—will find the negotiating landscape unaccommodating. Before securitized markets and the era of aggressive financial operators who focused on maximizing gains, a lender or an investor might have had an interest in helping a troubled business survive and thrive—but no more. Instead, Main Street will be roiling with mass layoffs, abrupt shutdowns of plants and divisions, and facilities left idle and unkempt while bankruptcy courts decide their fate.

Blackouts and shortages of food, water, fuel, medicines, and other necessities—even localized famines—will be a recurring problem. Adding to the misery will be fallout from trade wars, military hostilities, and other developments that will prevent domestic and global economies from functioning normally. During the later phase of the unraveling, hoarding will cause additional disruption. Managers whose business has been adversely affected by the collapse in demand and, of course, speculators, will look to make the most of dire circumstances, making matters worse.

Government policy distortions and infrastructure breakdowns, including collapsed bridges and tunnels, failing sewer and water systems, and roads rendered virtually unusable by a lack of maintenance, will add to the chaotic sense of an America under siege. So will more frequent accidents at run-down public facilities as well as environmental mishaps when public and private decision makers mistakenly cut too many corners.

Pressured to treat mounting numbers of patients with little or no health insurance and faced with severe cutbacks in funding, more and more hospitals and immediate-care facilities will be forced to close or limit access to treatment for large cross-sections of the population. But with many individuals and families already living in squalid circumstances without proper nutrition, the groundwork will be laid for a health disaster that sees overall life expectancy falling sharply, infant mortality increasing to centuries-old levels, and contagious diseases running rampant.

Oppressed by a pervasive sense of foreboding and hopelessness, growing numbers of Americans will turn to religion and spiritual alternatives in search of meaning and support. Mysticism, cults, and movements that promise contentment in the postphysical world will hold out great promise. Unfortunately, at least some of these groups, along with many mainstream religions, will end up poisoned by the same divisiveness and vulnerability to despotic overthrow that unsettle the secular landscape.

Many people will seek other diversions from the oppressive routine of everyday life, including virtual reality games and other escapist fare. The most popular forms of entertainment will either glorify the dark and seamy sides of life or will feature imagery that is at the polar opposite to a sad and somber existence. As during prior periods of economic turmoil, ruthless outlaws will vie with sweet heroines for the attentions of the masses. No small number of Americans will indulge in drugs or alcohol or other vices, or they will immerse themselves in a haze of partying and wild excess. Sadly, some of those who can't find temporary respite from life's travails will choose an altogether different way out, pushing suicide rates higher.

Instead of finding an escape route, some people will focus their energies on ferreting out and punishing those who they believe are behind the way things are. Rumors and reports of witch hunts, vigilantism, and "star chambers"—secret courts that mete out arbitrary justice—will crop up with disturbing frequency, further undermining respect for authority. Yet as civil unrest grows and talk of a broader, more dramatic change in the world order begins to circulate on the Internet and elsewhere, authorities, especially at the federal level, will crack down. Domestic surveillance activity will jump dramatically. State workers and local political groups will be called upon to monitor subversive chatter and identify key agitators. Laws will be drafted limiting many basic rights, including freedom of expression. Severe penalties will be imposed on those who openly criticize the government.

With police budgets severely constrained, municipal governments will increasingly turn to Washington for help. In spite of economic pressures, expanding legions of active duty and reserve military forces will be sent to trouble spots around the country and granted nearly absolute authority to restore order. In some places, vast detention camps will spring up, designed to handle a large influx of lawbreakers, troublemakers, and immigrants, illegal or otherwise, who will increasingly be seen as an unacceptable threat to national security.

Where there is local resistance, force and other aggressive measures will be justified in the name of preventing "foreign agents," or terrorists, from gaining a foothold on U.S. soil, and even mild dissent will frequently trigger dramatic responses. Amid a continued savaging of the social fabric, fears of martial law will intermingle with talk of revolution and secession. By then, what was once the land of the free and the home of the brave will be no more.

Chapter

12

GEOPOLITICAL

"Endless money forms the sinews of war."
—Cicero

According to surveys, nearly 80 percent of Japanese consumers believe that rice grown in California is inferior to the domestic variety. Those perceptions help to justify trade restrictions on an important and traditional dietary staple in that nation. But in a 2003 study featuring blind taste tests, 161 Japanese nationals were asked to rate characteristics such as sweetness, stickiness, texture, fragrance, and whiteness in both domestic and imported versions of the rice preferred in Japanese cooking—and most could not tell the difference. According to Ken Chinen, a professor of business at California State University in Sacramento and a native of Japan who oversaw the study, it was "just an issue of perception. Rice is rice."

Of course, nothing is that straightforward when it comes to protecting what are considered to be vital national interests. Indeed the Land of the Rising Sun relies on quotas, tariffs, unique standards, onerous testing procedures, restricted market access, and government procurement policies to limit imports of foreign rice. Such measures are not unique to Japan, however, and barriers protecting domestic markets will surely multiply in strength and number in the years ahead.

The shift will reflect a dramatic turnaround in the multidecade march toward globalization, as faltering growth and widespread financial and social upheaval induce governments everywhere to fence domestic economies away from unfolding turmoil. Despite those efforts, collapsing demand in the United States will reverberate far and wide, especially in regions such as Asia, which have become overly dependent on seemingly insatiable American consumer spending. China, which together with the United States accounted for about half of the world's gross domestic product growth from 2001 through 2005, will almost certainly endure an economic hard landing of its own as the twin bubbles of real estate and business investment collapse with a bang.

With the United States losing its place at the head of the economic table, the energizing force that has long led the charge for open markets and free trade will itself retreat into isolation and protectionism. In fact, the American public, spurred by feelings of anxiety, fear, distrust, and paranoia, will likely raise a growing clamor for barbwire and poured concrete as well as legal barriers. The turnaround in attitudes toward porous borders and the disintegration of one of the world's leading marketplaces for other nations' goods and services will parallel anti-American sentiment sweeping across the globe. For many, America's long-time paternalistic arrogance and self-appointed role as global police officer, economic authoritarian, and enforcer of the Judeo-Christian ethic was seen as tolerable only when others either stood to benefit or had little choice.

But with the cult of consumerism crumbling, the economy in a tailspin, the nation's financial system being consumed from within, public finances in tatters, and military resources stretched to the breaking point, outsiders will no longer have an incentive to ignore the new reality: the end of American hegemony.

Economic and financial shocks will reverberate back and forth between rich and poor, allies and adversaries, producers and consumers, and mature and developing nations. A siege mentality will take hold, where survival and gaining an advantage are the primary goals and "every man for himself" becomes the guiding principle.

As time goes on, the United States will lose ever more control over its own destiny, especially in economic and financial matters, a development already apparent in the years after the 1990's boom ended and the equity bubble burst. In the international energy markets, for example, prices and supply-demand dynamics were increasingly dominated by speculative interests and governments operating in hotspots around the world. In the financial markets, monetary policy changes in Japan, Europe, and China often had a more pronounced effect than did the activities of the Federal Reserve.

The war in Iraq and other military operations, which involved spending more than $500 billion per year, will become untenable burdens. They will also foment widespread anti-Americanism and growing calls to send U.S. troops home and leave the responsibility to others. With America's diminishing role on the world stage will come a reappraisal of many points of contention that were either discounted or ignored when other nations depended on the United States for their good fortune.

Signs of a shift were already apparent in the summer of 2006 amid the collapse of the Doha round of global trade negotiations, initiated at the behest of the United States after the 2001 terrorist attacks on the World Trade Center. In the end, the failure came down to bitter and continuing disputes over farm subsidies and a raft of tariff measures, as well as a "widening gap between America and others over what the round should achieve," according to *The Economist.* All of a sudden, more was to be gained from resisting American impetus for multilateral global accords and focusing instead on the benefits of self-sufficiency and regional alliances. For no small number of interested parties, the appropriate endgame was a world split into self-contained, protectionist trading blocks, resembling in some respects the original vision of a European Union with its porous internal borders and common currency.

This reassessment and realignment of international interests, together with a diminished respect for the United States' role as global agenda setter, underscored another transformation that was under way. In a July 2006 article, "Russia-U.S. Shift in Power Balance May Mold Summit," the *Wall Street Journal* notes that the Bush administration's decision to allow Russia to store spent nuclear fuel ahead of a gathering of top nations reflected a "shifting power balance between a United States facing challenges on several fronts and a Russia moving to reassert itself on the world stage."

The United States is also losing the ability to influence alliances it might once have anchored or refused to sanction. Based on common economic, social, religious, or environmental interests, nations such as Russia and China, Venezuela and North Korea, and even Iran and Iraq are finding potentially dangerous common ground. No small number of commentators also note that years of relatively strong economic performance in Asia has spurred a shift in influence from West to East. A period of rising commodity prices, aided in large part by a massive consumption boom in China, has swung the balance in favor of resource producers such as Iran, Venezuela, and Russia.

In many cases, unstable regimes are no longer willing to play second fiddle to the clique of leading nations such as the Group of Eight. Instead, they are vying to assume what they believe is their rightful place at the center of the global power nexus. Increasingly, they assert their rights to protect their own strategic national interests, and they seek to regain control of valuable resources, either through nationalization or expropriation, by claiming that outsiders are exploiting these resources.

Aided by sizable cash hordes and spurred by the need to source reliable and plentiful supplies of energy and raw materials, many of the economically awakened nations also seek to invest in businesses and markets outside their own borders. But those efforts have triggered backlashes from the United States. In 2005, for example, the Chinese National Petroleum Corporation voluntarily withdrew its bid for energy company Unocal at the request of the White House following a public outcry. Several months later, a hullabaloo erupted over government-owned Dubai World's bid to acquire the Peninsular and Oriental Steam Navigation Company, which held contracts to manage six U.S.-based port facilities.

In the wake of such moves, legislators in Washington scrambled to introduce measures that would change the process for reviewing foreign investments in the United States, especially those involving state-owned companies and that would allow authorities to keep closer tabs on what nonresident investors were up to. But frictions over trade and investment weren't the only points of contention. When China's economy was expanding at a double-digit pace and its rapidly rising output was absorbing an ever-greater share of the American import bill, the Asian nation also faced unwelcome pressure from the United States and elsewhere to revalue its currency, the yuan, which many believed was fixed at an artificially low level relative to the dollar.

No doubt many of these difficulties can be traced to America's structural deficiencies and external imbalances, which include large current account and budget deficits that worsen by the day. There is also the issue of the trillions of dollars held by those outside our shores—most of whom have no natural interest in the currency. For the better part of three decades, the United States ran a current account deficit, an excess of imports and current payments over exports and current earnings. This was the result of a declining manufacturing base, a rapidly expanding thirst for energy that could only be produced elsewhere, and an unhealthy predilection for foreign-made goods. By 2005, imports were more than 16 percent of gross domestic product, up from less than 6 percent only three decades earlier. When the trade deficit climbed to 6.6 percent of GDP by the second quarter of 2006, it had reached a dangerous stage. Americans had spent way more than they could afford for far too long and had relied on a staggering amount of borrowed money to pay for it, with much of the financing coming from foreigners.

As attitudes toward the United States change, more foreigners will question the dollar's longstanding role as a global reserve currency and international unit of account, especially when they realize how many of these paper promises have actually been created and put into circulation. Moreover, those who might once have had an interest in continuing to hold the currency and perhaps to add to the $13 trillion of stocks, bonds, factories, and other American assets that foreigners owned at the end of 2005 will reconsider. In a world of intense competition, heightened protectionism, and collapsing consumer demand, they will no longer have the same incentive to support the greenback and invest in America as an adjunct to an export-driven strategy as they did during the upswing.

Already in 2006, there were signs of a sea change. After years of massive purchases, some overseas holders began to diversify out of dollar-denominated securities. In March, the *Wall Street Journal* wrote that net foreign purchases of U.S. government securities fell 86 percent to a three-year low, while central banks were net sellers for the first time in a year. Other reports noted that the greenback was becoming increasingly vulnerable to a reshuffle of dollar reserves by Mideast and Asian nations. With foreigners holding more than 40 percent of U.S. Treasury bonds, 25 percent of outstanding corporate bonds, and 12 percent of corporate equities, the prospect of an abrupt, widespread exodus could only add to a dismal outlook for domestic securities' prices.

More than a few foreign countries also seek to diversify out of the dollar into precious metals and other assets. Russian President Vladimir Putin, for instance, reportedly ordered the nation's central bank in 2006 to boost gold's share of its $277 billion of foreign reserves from 5 to 10 percent, while China, which held only 1.4 percent of reserves in the precious metal, according to the World Gold Council, was being urged by domestic officials to increase its exposure. There has also been persistent and growing chatter, led by anti-American oil producers such as Iran and Venezuela, about changing the reference price for crude oil from dollars to euros, or even to units of gold, per barrel.

As sentiment toward the United States changes for the worse, the advantages of a widely held and readily tradable but intrinsically worthless and suddenly depreciating dollar will quickly be lost, transforming a once desirable asset into a liability. Along with this realization will come what many observers have long feared: a rapid and disorderly unwinding of existing global imbalances— and a plunge in the dollar.

Still, although little doubt exists about the longer term outlook for the greenback, especially given that U.S. officials will eventually be forced to turn on the monetary spigot full blast, the dollar may well swing noticeably higher versus other currencies in the short run. The combination of massive speculative bets against the currency; widespread margin calls at major financial intermediaries as volatile markets boost collateral requirements; unexpectedly tight monetary policy; and frantic efforts to convert assets of all kinds into cash to service trillions in dollar-denominated loans, bonds, and other obligations will likely trigger a short-term boost in demand.

These moves will ultimately prove unsustainable, however, as the wholesale destruction of purchasing power amid a hyperactive increase in the supply of the currency proves overwhelming. With the Fed eventually seeking to monetize anything and everything in sight, those who can will do their utmost to bail out of American currency. Dollar-denominated assets of all kinds, including former safe-haven investments such as Treasury bills and the debts of Fannie Mae and Freddie Mac, belatedly recognized as unbacked by government guarantee, will come under relentless selling pressure.

Markets will also suffer from the violent aftershocks of a dramatic increase in capital flight, as the remaining wealthy Americans and exposed foreigners try to exit before the door slams completely shut. A rash of financial problems, bank failures, legal proceedings, arbitrary decrees, and rising concern over a government that seems to have abdicated any semblance of fiscal discipline will further exacerbate those fears.

Many will wonder whether the United States might renege on some of its financial obligations or even declare an outright default on its once AAA securities. Likely adding to a widespread sense of panic will be the exodus from an array of global fiat currencies into gold, silver, property, and other tangible assets, which can hold their value in a world of government finances run amok. Needless to say, systemic financial pressures and domino-like bank failures will make preservation of capital the utmost concern.

Rising angst will also wreak havoc with links among markets, financial systems, economies, and countries. Many people could find themselves subject to stricter government controls or even find avenues closed off as a result of attempts to stem contagion effects. The widespread urge to withdraw will feed rising xenophobia, already inflamed by illegal immigration, unfair trade practices, and leaking borders. Playing to populist sentiment, politicians around the country will respond enthusiastically to calls for restrictions on foreigners. This will further feed a brain drain, as scientists, students, and other temporary visa holders are left with little choice but to uproot and go elsewhere, further sapping America's economic resiliency.

Continuing calls for curbs on the flow of finance and trade will inspire the United States and other nations to spew forth protectionist legislation like the notorious Smoot-Hawley bill. Introduced at the start of the Great Depression, it triggered a series of tit-for-tat economic responses, which many commentators believe helped turn a serious economic downturn into a prolonged and devastating global disaster. But if history is any guide, those lessons will have been long forgotten during the next collapse. Eventually, fed by a mood of desperation and growing public anger, restrictions on trade, finance, investment, and immigration will almost certainly intensify.

Authorities and ordinary citizens will likely scrutinize the cross-border movement of Americans and outsiders alike, and lawmakers may even call for a general crackdown on nonessential travel. Meanwhile, many nations will make transporting or sending funds to other countries exceedingly difficult. As desperate officials try to limit the fallout from decades of ill-conceived, corrupt, and reckless policies, they will introduce controls on foreign exchange. Foreign individuals and companies seeking to acquire certain American infrastructure assets, or trying to buy property and other assets on the cheap thanks to a rapidly depreciating dollar, will be stymied by limits on investment by noncitizens. Those efforts will cause spasms to ripple across economies and markets, disrupting global payment, settlement, and clearing mechanisms. All of this will, of course, continue to undermine business confidence and consumer spending.

In a world of lockouts and lockdowns, any link that transmits systemic financial pressures across markets through arbitrage or portfolio-based risk management, or that allows diseases to be easily spread from one country to the next by tourists and wildlife, or that otherwise facilitates unwelcome exchanges of any kind will be viewed with suspicion and dealt with accordingly.

The rise in isolationism and protectionism will bring about ever more heated arguments and dangerous confrontations over shared sources of oil, gas, and other key commodities as well as factors of production that must, out of necessity, be acquired from less-than-friendly nations. Whether involving raw materials used in strategic industries or basic necessities such as food, water, and energy, efforts to secure adequate supplies will take increasing precedence in a world where demand seems constantly out of kilter with supply. Disputes over the misuse, overuse, and pollution of the environment and natural resources will become more commonplace. Around the world, such tensions will give rise to full-scale military encounters, often with minimal provocation.

In some instances, economic conditions will serve as a convenient pretext for conflicts that stem from cultural and religious differences. Alternatively, nations may look to divert attention away from domestic problems by channeling frustration and populist sentiment toward other countries and cultures. Enabled by cheap technology and the waning threat of American retribution, terrorist groups will likely boost the frequency and scale of their horrifying attacks, bringing the threat of random violence to a whole new level.

Turbulent conditions will encourage aggressive saber rattling and interdictions by rogue nations running amok. Age-old clashes will also take on a new, more heated sense of urgency. China will likely assume an increasingly belligerent posture toward Taiwan, while Iran may embark on overt colonization of its neighbors in the Mideast. Israel, for its part, may look to draw a dwindling list of allies from around the world into a growing number of conflicts. Some observers, like John Mearsheimer, a political scientist at the University of Chicago, have even speculated that an "intense confrontation" between the United States and China is "inevitable" at some point.

More than a few disputes will turn out to be almost wholly ideological. Growing cultural and religious differences will be transformed from wars of words to battles soaked in blood. Long-simmering resentments could also degenerate quickly, spurring the basest of human instincts and triggering genocidal acts. Terrorists employing biological or nuclear weapons will vie with conventional forces using jets, cruise missiles, and bunker-busting bombs to cause widespread destruction. Many will interpret stepped-up conflicts between Muslims and Western societies as the beginnings of a new world war.

As events unfold, unsettling geopolitical tensions and the continuing economic collapse will weigh heavily on the familiar routines of everyday life, forcing many Americans to wonder when, or if, it will ever end.

DEFENSES

13

PLANNING

"A man should learn to sail in all winds."
—Italian Proverb

A prolific writer renowned for his insights on creativity, Edward de Bono is credited with pioneering the concept of "lateral thinking," which relies on deliberate methods and fresh perspectives to solve difficult problems. In his 1968 book *New Think: The Use of Lateral Thinking in the Generation of New Ideas,* de Bono offers the example of a merchant forced to wager the hand of his daughter in marriage against the payment of a large debt to a repulsive moneylender. As part of the bargain, she must pick one of two different-colored stones from a bag. If she chooses black, she will become the moneylender's wife and the debt will be canceled. If she chooses white, neither she nor her father will have any further obligation.

The daughter notices, however, that the moneylender has secretly placed two black stones into the bag; thus, she faces a dilemma. If she makes a selection, she will have no choice but to marry the usurer. If she refuses, her father will end up in prison. Eventually, the daughter chooses a stone, but without looking at it, allows it to fumble from her hand and mix with others lying on the ground. Cleverly, she says to the moneylender that if he looks at the color of the stone that remains in the bag, he will know which one she picked.

Such resourcefulness will be necessary in an era of unfamiliar conditions, unexpected developments, and constant upheaval—when economic and social conditions deteriorate rapidly, the financial system rips apart at the seams, markets are in turmoil, interest rates trend higher, and terrorism and geopolitical conflict become a tragic daily reality.

The times will call for judicious planning and decision making. The carefree spending and boundless optimism of earlier decades must, as a matter of course, be replaced by discretion, deliberation, and diligence. Instead of living for today and forgetting about tomorrow, or borrowing too much and saving too little, Americans will have to hunker down and steel themselves for a protracted period of hardship and suffering. With the economic pie shrinking fast, it will be a time to think small; to simplify, consolidate, and downsize; and to weed out anything that might, in one way or another, be unnecessary or even a threat to survival.

Historically, the three largest household expenditures have been shelter, food, and transportation. Those categories will almost certainly be the primary focus of attention early in the coming crisis, though as circumstances worsen, budgetary concerns won't end there. For some, cutting back might mean eliminating faux necessities, such as dining out or leaving the heating or air conditioning on in empty rooms. For the majority of Americans, however, choices will likely be far more difficult—leading in many cases to painful sacrifices.

People who underestimate the severity of the dangers ahead and fail to take the necessary steps at the outset risk being left penniless. Americans must scrutinize everything and anything that has to do with money and finance, from budgets and attitudes to habits and standards. Day in and day out, individuals and businesses must ask questions like, "Can it be done cheaper?" or, "Are there more efficient alternatives?" or, "Which features are really necessary?"

When the time comes to spend, earn, or save, people must take the initiative and alter their approach. Hard times will require a dramatic change in mind-set, from passive acceptance to an aggressive and exclusive focus on one's self-interest. Then, once a decision has been made, the next step will to be to carry it out—ruthlessly and efficiently. That decision might include haggling and haranguing; engaging in exhaustive research; rejiggering the timing of purchases to capitalize on ordering, seasonal, and retail cycles; or simply learning to say no, at least during the initial stages of the unraveling

For most people, what lies ahead will present an enormous intellectual, psychological, and emotional challenge, with conditions varying from depression and systemic crisis to hyperinflation and even full-scale economic collapse. In an environment where economic activity and prices fall sharply, delaying purchases and adopting an aggressive selling posture is the most appropriate course of action. The opposite holds true, however, when the prices of goods and services are spiraling higher and the nation's currency is rapidly losing value.

When asset prices crumble under the weight of violent deleveraging and an abrupt shift in risk preferences, the motto must be "Cash is king." But if hyperinflation runs rampant, one of the biggest mistakes is to hold cash and allow it to remain idle, even for a day. One must spend it as quickly as possible, either on tangible assets such as precious metals, commodities, or property—all of which retain some measure of their purchasing power—or on necessities such as food, fuel, or medicine that will cost more later and may be subject to shortages.

Still, knowing the appropriate steps to take under different scenarios isn't necessarily enough if the reporting lags and complexities of a sprawling global economy obscure signals when to favor one approach over the other.

Yet some strategies can make the going easier. For one thing, it will be wise to pay heed to at least one timeless maxim: "Assume the worst, hope for the best, and be prepared for whatever happens." Coping when many people are trapped beneath the rubble of an irresponsible or impetuous past will call for considerable courage, stamina, and resolve, which must come from within. Constant turmoil and heightened uncertainty about the future will require "What if?" thinking and the ability to anticipate situations that used to be rare or nonexistent. Another key is to be flexible and open-minded, especially with regard to previously low-probability events. With economic, financial, geopolitical, and social spheres in a turbulent state, dangerous chasms could easily open anywhere.

Under nearly all scenarios, the best strategy will be to reduce obligations and add resources. That means eliminating liabilities, or at least the more egregious risks associated with borrowing money and accumulating assets. The exact structure of holdings must be dictated by personal circumstances and economic prospects. Moreover, individuals and firms must not only try to forecast future needs but also anticipate what might be available and when, as well as how it can be secured. That is a daunting task to be sure, but scrambling for goods and services when budgets are tight and shortages widespread will be a luxury few can afford.

Americans will have little choice but to think clearly, stay informed, be organized, and plan effectively. Good planning, of course, makes sense in most circumstances, especially when finances or investments are involved. Placing too much faith on being "fast on your feet" could be risky, and the cost of avoidable mistakes could prove fatal.

For many people, an effective preparation strategy will involve creating a planning portfolio that not only takes into account issues such as spending and saving but also addresses a full range of related concerns, such as health care needs, insurance, and longer-term security. Ideally, such a portfolio will consist of three parts: a realistic budget that monitors and helps control spending, a financial plan geared toward a focused restructuring of the personal balance sheet, and an investment strategy that serves as a road map for protecting and enhancing overall wealth.

There will be overlaps. Spending categories, for example, must feature an allocation for savings, whereas strategies to generate extra funds, such as selling off unused personal assets or developing a home-based business, should be included too. Planning must also address the impact of higher income, property, sales, and other taxes during the first phase of the unraveling.

But good planning skills will not be enough to cope with the coming hard times. Americans will also have to develop a nose for danger, a kind of personal radar that can quickly alert them to potentially negative developments. More than ever, the forewarned will be forearmed. To a great extent, an awareness of potential threats involves paying close attention to local, national, and international news with an emphasis on the unusual, the extreme, or the unfamiliar. As Sherlock Holmes observes in the Sir Arthur Conan Doyle mystery "The Adventure of Silver Blaze," it will be critical to listen to the sounds of dogs that do not bark. The ability to ask pertinent and probing questions, as well as engage in a process of due diligence to mitigate at least some of the risks associated with chaotic times, will be invaluable.

Employees and entrepreneurs will have little choice but to stay on top of sector and industry trends, as well as any information or intelligence regarding strategy, direction, policy, and personnel, by monitoring specialized publications, news channels, and Web sites. Hearsay and rumors will likely serve as a valuable resource when failures, chicanery, and criminal activity rise dramatically. Fresh insights can also be gained by sifting through contrasting and, perhaps, extremist views from those at either end of the ideological and moral spectrum. Even though much of the material may be worthless, there will be occasional nuggets of valuable truth.

Fortunately, uncovering useful intelligence may involve nothing more than tapping into resources that are already widely available, increasingly by way of the Internet. These include foreign or alternative news sources such as *www.bbc.co.uk*, *www.economist.com*, *http://drudgereport.com*, or *http://rense.com*, *www.whatreallyhappened.com*, among others. Stories buried in the backs of newspapers and their online complements, such as the *Wall Street Journal*, the *New York Times*, and similar publications will likely prove highly informative as well.

So might news and information derived from news portals, blogs, and other modern-day digital channels that can be targeted directly, either through search engines or by using what are known as "aggregators," like Bloglines, described in detail later. Up-to-the-minute data and a real-time awareness of what is unfolding across the seven continents will be critical in an environment where fear and uncertainty reign. By using the resources available at *www.google.com, www.yahoo.com, www.msn.com*, and the Web sites of various content providers, including "news alert" features that allow topics of interest to be tracked in real time, staying informed need not be extraordinarily difficult.

Paradoxically, the Internet also holds vast stores of propaganda and information that has been altered or manipulated in some way, often by those with an axe to grind. But rather than obscuring the truth, alternative, reactionary, and even bizarre perspectives can sometimes help to extract the essence of what is really going on, like scenes viewed through more than one lens. Indeed, with economic, financial, social, and geopolitical conditions likely to become unglued nearly everywhere, not accepting anything at face value will be crucial. The world as we know it will be under siege; truth may well be the first casualty.

No doubt there will be plenty of extraneous noise. The mass media, for example, will probably paint a picture of what is unfolding that might best be described as manic-depressive. Politicians and others with a vested interest will try to engage in censorship, whether overtly or behind the scenes, disseminating virtually continuous propaganda: everything is under control, and there is light at the end of the tunnel. At the same time, economic and financial turmoil, increasing crime and revelations about past frauds, and a rapidly souring social mood will spur investigative and other reporting that borders on rabid bloodlust.

Listening, reading, paying attention, and thinking clearly will offer other benefits. By knowing what options are available, people will be able to negotiate from a position of strength rather than weakness, a critical advantage in a resource-constrained environment. Awareness of one's own and others' emotional states will prove especially useful when conditions are highly charged and anxiety, fear, denial, and panic are running riot. Like traders, people must be willing to act independently, change direction in a heartbeat, admit mistakes without undue worry or embarrassment, overcome peer pressure and resentment, and move past the need for ego gratification to stay ahead of the game.

Many people will be either largely on their own or will depend on a tight circle of trusted relationships. The vast majority of brokers, bankers, accountants, and other traditional advisors will be blind to the harsh realities of a dramatically changing economic landscape. Moreover, they and others will be so focused on their own legal, financial, or personal woes that they will be in no position to offer timely, consistent, or suitably unbiased advice.

With economic circumstances undermining the social fabric and opportunistic crime becoming increasingly widespread, Americans will have to be on the lookout for those who seek to take advantage. Sadly, the watchwords will increasingly be "Better safe than sorry." People will need to scrutinize everything that can affect them and their finances and keep an eye peeled for inconsistencies and omissions. More so than before, conditions will dictate that people take careful and exhaustive stock of what they have and what they don't, where they are and where they are headed, what is essential and what is superfluous, and how they will cope in a world seemingly gone mad.

Those who are employed must take whatever steps are necessary to try to stay employed. That means playing the corporate games; keeping up-to-date with what is going on in the company, the industry, and the economy; and honing technical, interpersonal, and other key skills. Even so, many of those who have a job at the outset of the coming economic disaster will quickly find themselves out on the street as conditions deteriorate. Falling demand, rising interest rates, growing trade wars, a depressing outlook—all will take their toll on headcounts, causing unemployment to soar.

Although it might seem like tempting fate, sometimes the best way to plan ahead under such circumstances is to assume that things will turn out badly. This makes especially good sense for individuals who work in the consumer goods sector and industries like housing and finance, which will be thoroughly wracked by the debacle. Firms and industries that were already in precarious shape, especially airlines and the auto-related sector with their large legacy costs and unfunded pension exposures, will also be extremely risky places at which to work or with whom to do business.

The fallout from complicated financial engineering and organizations that were not built to last will be a constant source of destructive energy. Virtually any business or industry might end up in dire straits, if not directly, then from a domino-like collapse following the failure of key suppliers, credit providers, and other counterparties. Under the circumstances, efforts that address the revenue side of the personal finance equation should include constant networking, updating résumés, developing preplanned job searches, engaging in ongoing marketplace assessments, and taking concrete steps to enhance and expand skill sets. Securing additional education or training in related fields and exploring alternative or secondary career options should also be part of the process.

Odds are, however, that the operating environment will become so hostile that securing an income will increasingly depend on cultivating an entrepreneurial spirit. Diminishing social and financial safety nets combined with a massive scramble for survival as the disaster drags on will also enhance the value of having some means of self-sufficiency.

The years ahead will hold other threats to well-being and security. The private pension system will be a far cry from what it used to be, if it even exists at all, while Social Security will almost certainly have little to offer for most of today's workers. Those who haven't managed to provide for their own future will discover that the official retirement age, which will likely be pushed back by at least ten years over the next few decades, will be little more than a milestone that marks another phase of life on the job. Health care coverage will also be in short supply, and those without insurance will be forced to rely on dwindling private charity, personal networks, or self-treatment. Repositories of expert knowledge and other resources available at little or no cost on the Internet may be the only alternative.

The best approach to the coming crisis will involve a plan that coordinates budgeting and investment oriented toward the accumulation of assets and long-term economic independence. It should also have built-in protection against a wide range of threats to economic well-being and security. This will include auto, health, property, and life insurance, which should be assessed in light of changing economic circumstances. Aside from legally mandated coverage, insurance should serve primarily as a backstop to catastrophic loss, with high deductibles and consequently lower premiums. Amounts that otherwise would have been spent on premiums should be added to emergency reserves.

Besieged by financial pressures, insurers are likely to revoke many existing policies following claims. In some cases, cancellations will come even in the absence of misfortune, as entire underwriting lines or geographic regions are eliminated because of losses. Many policies will offer less value for the money. Rising red ink, falling investment returns, and growing counterparty woes will leave numerous insurers at risk of failing themselves. Under the circumstances, they will inevitably boost premiums, scale back coverage, and take a much harder line about honoring the terms of outstanding policies.

Planning must take into account this new reality. Careful attention should be paid to ensuring that policies are up-to-date, learning all contract terms, making payments on time, securing acknowledgment that funds have been received, and monitoring the financial health of insurers. Strategic diversification of household assets and liabilities as well as financial, economic, and social relationships will also be necessary.

Americans must also take steps to prepare for the eventual divestment out of the dollar prior to its wholesale collapse, whether into other, presumably more stable currencies or into precious metals, commodities, property, and assorted tangible assets. Apart from the mechanics of conversion, planning should also address practical and logistical concerns, including opening accounts and making storage, insurance, and other necessary arrangements.

Political developments will likely be a dangerous wild card that can play havoc with personal finances. Although all sorts of taxes will be pushed higher, at least until a taxpayer revolt picks up steam, a breakdown in the economic and social order will likely trigger a potentially more costly response, including the revocation of civil liberties and various other restrictions. From limits on cash holdings and withdrawals to forced conversions of savings and mutual fund accounts, to banking "holidays," to confiscations and bans on ownership of certain kinds of assets, including gold and silver, to restrictions on travel and even martial law, the odds of drastic actions taking place will grow by the day.

Last but not least, proper planning should also anticipate a range of potential disasters, whether natural, like earthquakes and hurricanes, or human-made. Files should be backed up, using off-site storage if possible, while important documents, account numbers, medical information, insurance photos and inventories, and the like should be kept in secure, readily accessible locations. The period ahead will be a time of profound change and constant turmoil, and survival will depend on staying informed, being prepared, and planning accordingly.

14

INVESTMENTS

"Save a little money each month, and at the end of the year,
You'll be surprised at how little you have."

—Ernest Haskins

At the end of 1979, Bunker and Herbert Hunt seemed to be on top of the world. In less than three months, silver had doubled to more than $34 per ounce, the shorts were being squeezed mercilessly, and the billionaires were growing richer by the day. That is because the Hunt brothers owned 40 million ounces of silver between them and 90 million ounces jointly through a company they had formed with two Saudi sheiks several months earlier. The group also controlled futures contracts on another 90 million ounces, with delivery due in March.

However, on January 7 and again on January 21 of that year the Comex—Commodity Exchange of New York—changed the rules. First, they limited the size of futures positions that traders could hold to the equivalent of ten million ounces. Then, they announced that only liquidation orders would be permitted. Those two amendments, along with an aggressive Federal Reserve tightening that boosted the cost of financing inventory positions to uncomfortable levels, helped drive down the price of silver from a record high of $50 per ounce in mid-January to $21 two months later. By then, the Hunt brothers were on the hook for a $135 million margin call that they could not meet. It was the end of the road for their big foray into precious metals. Eight years later, the two men were convicted of trying to "corner" the silver market, and Bunker was forced to file for personal bankruptcy.

Although what happened nearly three decades ago might be viewed as a curious anomaly, the tumultuous period ahead likely will see rules changes, disruptions, and market closures that can suddenly transform substantial paper profits into equally large realized losses. In the wake of the 1987 stock market crash, for example, some of those who were lucky enough to have bet correctly on falling prices, either with put options or short positions in stocks or index futures, discovered that they could not cash in their chips, either because trading was temporarily halted or jammed phone lines made it impossible to get through to their brokers.

Largely discounted in recent years, rising illiquidity and problems stemming from counterparty, technology, and systemic failures will be a growing source of concern for small and large investors alike when markets are in turmoil, financial institutions are threatened with insolvency, and the fallout from an unwinding credit boom intensifies. In many respects, the period ahead can only call to mind the sobering words of legendary cowboy, author, and philosopher Will Rogers, who noted after the 1929 stock market crash: "I am not so much concerned with the return on capital as I am with the return of capital."

Indeed, at least some age-old wisdom will undoubtedly prove invaluable when the mistakes and excesses of the past come home to roost. Diversification will be essential, though not necessarily for the reasons usually cited by professional investment advisors. In a multiphase economic and financial meltdown, a broad range of asset classes will often gyrate wildly in sync, and spreading the risk will not necessarily smooth returns. Rather, diversification will preserve financial security in a world of recurring abrupt and unexpected implosions. In addition, assuming that fair prices—or any market at all—will be available for securities and assets could prove to be a serious error of judgment.

Other long-held notions will have to fall by the wayside. For a start, Americans will have to accept that the age of "buy and hold" is over. Simply surviving will demand the wiles of a trader, who relies on flexibility, keen awareness, and iron discipline. Of course, this doesn't mean that everyone should start speculating, "flipping," or day trading their way to financial freedom. Evaporating liquidity, surging volatility, and scads of confusing "noise" will mean that only the most seasoned operators will be able to capitalize on the chaos. Instead, it will be a time to reconsider the fool's game of hanging on and hoping that things work out for the best.

Changing circumstances will also signify that it's time to be bearish, favoring caution over exuberance and fearing a decline more than missing out on a rise. Rather than "buying the dip," Americans will need to focus on "selling the blip" before they are left with holdings that they do not want. Indeed, for most people, acquiring a solid grasp of how and when to sell will offer a significant advantage. Taking small but relatively manageable losses early on, thereby limiting the possibility of getting wiped out later, should be investment rule number one.

In a bear market, it is common to see violent rallies that offer a kind of olive branch of bullishness to those who have been hanging on in hopes of a turnaround. Individuals who remain attuned to the bigger picture can take advantage and use that volatility to liquidate or restructure their own holdings. As depressing as it sounds, those who wish to work through the treacherous times must take a continuing stand against premature and potentially dangerous feelings of optimism and complacency as well as the natural urge to engage in knee-jerk bargain hunting. Undoubtedly, catastrophes that were decades in the making will take a very long time to work themselves out.

More than before, Americans must be on guard against self-deception and unwarranted sanguinity, especially when feeling vulnerable makes them a gullible audience for fairy-tale endings and clouds with silver linings. A measure of paranoia and a healthy skepticism will go a long way when desperation and despair bring out the worst in people. Where advice is concerned, old-fashioned wisdom should apply: If what is offered is unsolicited or "free," or has come from a source that might have some sort of hidden agenda, then it will almost certainly be of little value. It also goes without saying that if something sounds too good to be true, then it almost certainly is.

People should be wary of taking anything at face value, because much of what they see will not be as it seems. Acquiring critical intelligence in a dangerous new world will depend on active research, careful analysis, and diligent follow-up. It will also mean asking all sorts of questions and trying to anticipate what can, and invariably will, go wrong. One place to look, funnily enough, will be the financial markets. Although the day-to-day disorder will not offer much insight, broad trends in stocks, bonds, currencies, and commodities will probably serve as divining rods for meaningful developments.

The fallout from multiple disasters will seem bewildering, requiring an exceptional combination of focus and detachment. From market shutdowns and abrupt failures, to nationalizations and confiscations, to the growing likelihood of world war and rapidly spreading social disorder—all will represent threats that in and of themselves could wipe out the ill-prepared. But critical intelligence won't be hard to find, especially with the power of the Internet at hand.

To ensure a well-rounded picture, reports from mainstream news sources should be supplemented with content gleaned from industry-, sector-, and theme-specific channels as well as newsletters and bearish or "alternative" Web sites like these:

http://prudentbear.com
http://safehaven.com

http://financialsense.com
http://dailyreckoning.com
www.fiendbear.com
www.bullnotbull.com/bull
www.24hgold.com

Certain blogs can also serve as a conduit to timely market, financial, economic, and geopolitical developments. Some of the best include these:

http://bigpicture.typepad.com
http://billcara.com
www.thekirkreport.com
http://seekingalpha.com
http://tradermike.net
http://globaleconomicanalysis.blogspot.com
http://themessthatgreenspanmade.blogspot.com

The most appropriate investment strategy will take into account potentially fast-changing economic and financial circumstances, which will run the gamut from economic contraction to runaway inflation and a collapse of the dollar. Americans will have to try to anticipate threats that could admittedly be hard for anyone to comprehend, let alone capitalize on.

Of course, every individual's situation being unique makes it all the more challenging to offer one-size-fits-all advice. Still, for most people becoming more self-aware, setting goals that are appropriate to personal circumstances, developing carefully crafted plans, and remaining disciplined will be essential. One's overriding philosophy must focus on long-term survival. This means safety, liquidity, and transparency should carry far more weight than the possibility of high yields or excess returns. Simplicity should be valued over complexity. "Plain vanilla" investments and approaches will generally prove better bets than those that are too difficult to execute or explain in more than one sentence. Strategies involving derivatives or the use of leverage should be avoided, unless the potential rewards far outweigh the many risks.

For the majority of Americans, the right approach will begin with getting their current finances in order and only then directing their attention to future returns. More than likely, that will mean focusing on the right side of the personal balance sheet, where the liabilities are found. Plain and simple, the near-term goal of many Americans must be to eliminate debt or, at the very least, to minimize the fallout from being overly exposed to the consequences of economic and financial upheaval. One risk is a full-scale credit crunch, in which it is virtually impossible to borrow money or refinance loans through any legitimate source. Another threat is a continuing structural rise in interest rates and risk premiums, which are the extra margins that creditors demand as compensation for increased uncertainty.

Again, the range of potential debt-reducing options will vary depending on individual circumstances, especially if real estate or other financed assets are involved. Yet the first step should be to undertake a clear assessment of the extent and makeup of exposure to borrowed money and which current and future resources can realistically be used to pay off existing obligations. Where options for full repayment are limited, consideration should be given to restructuring or refinancing outstanding borrowings, which might mean locking in lower rates or better terms or converting floating-rate debt into fixed-rate obligations. This initial effort should be followed, in any case, by the development of an amortization plan geared to paying off balances as quickly as possible.

Homeowners with mortgages and those with financed assets like cars or boats will have a crucial decision to make. They must determine whether the advantages of leveraged ownership outweigh the disadvantages, especially when liquidity disappears and valuations are under pressure. A personal balance sheet that is skewed in favor of being property rich and cash poor could become a ball and chain of financial serfdom. The investment and ATM-like attributes of home ownership will lose their relevance, replaced by the practical demands of everyday living.

In many respects, there will be no such thing as home equity during the first phase of economic unraveling. Not until later, when inflation is spiraling out of control, will ownership of tangible assets, like a home, be anything other than a lifestyle choice. With the extraordinary property bubble of recent years poised to deflate, people who sell fast and first are likely to see the least amount of damage. Later, the ranks of potential buyers will thin out, and the market will effectively disappear. Those who were unwilling or unable to exit before then will either be stuck with what they have or be forced to dump their interests, maybe for pennies on the dollar. Others will lose their homes to foreclosure, though when the ranks of defaulters swell dramatically, banks may be willing to work with borrowers and grant mortgage-payment holidays or forgive at least some debt to make the most of a disastrous situation.

While a window of opportunity exists, it makes sense to downsize, to sell immediately and rent instead, or to consider going without lifestyle accoutrements, such as a second car, that could become intolerable burdens. Unfortunately, those whose cash flow is inadequate or who are already in dire straits will have to weigh other, more drastic steps, including contacting consumer credit counseling agencies or lenders to work out a compromise. As a last resort, many Americans may have to consider walking away from their outstanding obligations or have them discharged through bankruptcy, even under the new, more draconian legal framework, in the interests of their longer-term security.

When it comes to the left side of the personal balance sheet, remaining flexible and maintaining a strong sense of discipline will be vitally important. Early on, few asset classes will be safe from the ravages of the bursting credit bubble. That includes, as mentioned earlier, virtually any type of real estate. Notoriously illiquid at the best of times and boosted to unsustainable heights by years of cheap money, reckless speculation, and greater-fool buying, both the commercial and residential property markets will be unmitigated disasters. The prices of precious metals and other commodities—perhaps even energy—will almost certainly suffer, too. A spike in risk premiums and a short-term boost in demand for U.S. dollars, as lenders anxiously call in loans, will also undercut demand, at least initially.

Under those circumstances, holding cash and its equivalents will be the most viable short-term strategy for most Americans. Traditionally, the range of available options has included physical currency; U.S. Treasury bills and short-maturity bonds; money market mutual funds; and FDIC-insured checking accounts, savings accounts, and certificates of deposit. But over time, a financial system under siege will require more selectivity. Many money market funds, especially those that invest in anything other than direct obligations of the U.S. government—such as the unguaranteed securities issued by GSEs like Fannie Mae and Freddie Mac—will be vulnerable to sharp sell-offs, while others may be at risk because of problems at sponsoring firms. And although insured bank deposits will retain their gilt-edged status in the short run, the fallout from multiple bank failures and a broadening systemic crisis will eventually strain the resources of the reserve fund. Odds are, in fact, that authorities will be forced to scale back or even eliminate deposit guarantees.

During past economic downturns, long-term, fixed-income securities were viewed as an attractive investment option. However, that view is unlikely to continue following a severe credit crunch; massive liquidation of bond positions held by banks and other highly leveraged operators; near-term boosts in federal, state, and local debt issuance in the wake of falling tax revenues; and an apparent reversal of a two-decade long downtrend in interest rates. These factors will place considerable pressure on prices, putting principal at risk. When hyperinflation sets in, the situation will be even worse. Historically, rapid increases in the price of goods and services and a collapsing currency have created the worst possible environment for investing in bonds and other fixed-payment obligations. Combine that with the prospect of liquidations by foreign holders and eventual downgrades in America's AAA debt rating, and the risks of owning long-maturity, fixed-income securities seriously outweigh any potential rewards.

Even U.S. Treasury Inflation-Protected Securities (TIPS), whose principal is ostensibly guaranteed to increase in line with overall price changes, will likely offer little real protection, as hyperinflation leads to changes in methodology or outright distortions in reported inflation data. Such a development would not be out of line with past practice. For example, during the 1990s, when compiling the monthly Consumer Price Index, the U.S. Bureau of Labor Statistics began using "hedonic" adjustments, where price rises for certain goods are arbitrarily discounted as improvements in quality, helping to mask the underlying level of inflation.

Corporate and municipal fixed-income securities are also not viable fixed-income alternatives. With the added threat of public and private sector finances and overall creditworthiness deteriorating sharply, these markets will be under constant selling pressure. Because of the difficulties of assessing default risk as multiple large-scale bankruptcies and systemic crises loom, the odds of getting it wrong will be too high for all but the most sophisticated and nimble investors.

For any number of reasons—not least of which is that valuations have a long history of "reverting to the mean"—the equity market is second only to real estate in terms of potential downside risk. As has always been the case with publicly traded shares, corporate profitability and perceived attractiveness has tended to ebb and flow, tracing out pendulum-like swings from pessimism and fear to optimism and exuberance and back again. By 2006, with profit margins at multidecade highs, dividend yields not far from all-time lows, and P/E ratios—stock price divided by earnings—at levels that had long signaled overvaluation, equities were at giddy heights and already vulnerable.

But with the economy rolling over, an increasingly hostile global monetary environment, liquidity and risk preferences undergoing a complete about-face, new rules exposing multibillion-dollar pension obligations and other off-balance-sheet risks, and a growing scandal involving corporate share options, prices were poised to go one way: down. As the great unraveling plays out, equities will come under relentless and often frantic selling pressure, interrupted only by relatively brief short-covering rallies and periods of calm-before-the-storm complacency.

The supply of stock will come from many quarters. These include hedge funds, brokers, and banks, many of which will be looking to exit leveraged positions and hedge derivative bets gone wrong; increasingly nervous individual and institutional investors, reacting to the growing spate of bad news; and buyout firms, which had used massive borrowing to take over public and private firms with an eye to floating them off or selling them later. Joining them will be the issuers themselves, as they suddenly become aware that the era of raising inexpensive capital through the equity markets is drawing to a close.

Especially vulnerable will be shares of companies already in sorry shape. Firms in sectors with significant exposure to real estate, consumer spending, and finance, as well as those with large pension, health care, and other "legacy" costs, will also be at risk. There will be few places to hide, though the common stock of larger companies will probably outperform those of smaller firms. Companies in traditionally defensive sectors, such as food and beverages, will tend to outpace those of other groups, as will shares with higher dividend yields, but only in relative terms.

For those who fully prepare themselves for the coming dangers, executing bearishly oriented investment strategies and trading specialized instruments that benefit from falling stock and bond prices may be a viable option. This approach could include buying bearishly oriented and "inverse" mutual funds and exchange-traded funds (ETFs); selling futures, shares, bonds, and other securities short; and buying put options. The costs of being wrong, however, could be prohibitive at a time of exploding volatility and nonlinear market shifts. In addition, the window of opportunity is sure to shrink fast as counterparty, operational, technological, and systemic crises boost the risks of being locked in without a means of escape.

No matter the approach, Americans must stay focused on where things are and where they are likely headed.

At some point, economic circumstances and foreign exchange markets will signal the need for a major shift in investment strategy. The dollar will lose momentum or begin to fall versus other major currencies, numerous reports will highlight reasons to be positive on the greenback—ironically indicating that its short-term zenith has been reached—and stories will surface of traders who have lost large sums betting on a fall. A more definitive signal, no doubt, will come when the dollar resumes its very long-term structural slide and the currency trades at new record lows versus the Swiss franc, the euro, and the yen.

Then it will be time to switch immediately out of dollars into other currencies and invest in precious metals. Although the various paper promises issued by governments around the world will all be suspect, the case for exchanging the dollar into other currencies can be characterized as a "relative value trade," or the lesser of two evils. Practically speaking, people will still need some convenient medium of exchange, which will naturally favor major currencies whose supply-and-demand fundamentals, among other things, are not as lopsidedly negative as they are for the greenback.

The best option, but also the riskiest in terms of security, will be to hold physical currency itself. Next in order of preference will be foreign currency accounts at highly rated overseas financial institutions based on the kinds of research described in the next chapter, as well as investments in Treasury bills and short-term bonds issued by countries with relatively strong finances. Bringing up the rear will be foreign-currency-denominated ETFs and mutual funds, overseas money market and short-term bond funds, and federally insured nondollar savings accounts and certificates of deposit at

U.S.-based banks. But in an era of rising counterparty and other risks, these latter options will become less feasible over time.

With the dollar's reversal to the downside also signaling that more transitory asset-liquidation pressures have been alleviated, gold and silver prices will be poised to resume their longer-term upward trajectory after what could be a rather substantial correction from 2006 highs. The case for investing in precious metals, of course, rests on their rarity value and the fact that humankind's ability to produce gold and silver has more or less tracked overall economic development through the years. As such, these metals are seen as a form of wealth that tends to maintain its purchasing power, unlike fiat currencies such as the dollar.

While the purest way to accumulate gold and silver is in bullion form, this strategy has drawbacks, including transportation logistics; the need for storage, safekeeping, and assaying; and related costs. There is also the matter of the bars' inherent bulkiness, especially when accumulating significant stockpiles. Owning gold and silver coins, however, can address at least some of those concerns. The South African Krugerrand, which has traditionally been priced at a modest premium to its precious metal content, and the American Eagle and Canadian Maple Leaf, which have usually garnered a greater markup, are readily exchangeable and generally do not need to have their purity assessed.

Other alternatives include gold and silver warehouse receipts and exchange-traded funds listed in the United States and elsewhere, as well as the individual shares, ETFs, mutual funds, and other instruments that are tied to the fortunes of mining companies. Gold- and silver-backed currencies, such as the Islamic dinar, as well as "digital" variants including e-gold, GoldMoney, and e-bullion are also available. In the early stages of dollar decline, indirect ownership may represent a reasonable compromise in terms of convenience and security. But as circumstances deteriorate, the potential for fraud, bankruptcy, and various other counterparty risks will grow, making the trade-off more precarious.

And because they are equities, mining company stocks also will be vulnerable to the liquidation pressures affecting share prices overall, as well as to fundamental operating factors such as rising interest rates, which will impact most businesses and sectors. Geopolitical developments, including terrorist activities or moves to nationalize mining assets—which might, ironically enough, boost the price of the commodities in question—will also be a threat. Eventually, attitudes about gold and silver mining shares will change. Rather than being viewed as equities, they will be valued based on the businesses of the underlying companies and the assets they control.

More than likely, that transition will come about as monetary expansion moves into overdrive and hyperinflation gets under way. By then, circumstances will require another, far more dramatic mind-set shift. When central bankers are cranking up the monetary presses, most of the so-called "prudent " rules will need to be turned on their heads. In such an environment, nothing is to be gained from caution and restraint. Rather, it is a time to spend cash and savings as fast as possible, either on necessary items that will undoubtedly cost more tomorrow or on tangible assets whose prices will keep pace with the overall trend. Historically, runaway inflation has been accompanied by frantic buying of gold and silver as well as real estate and various hard goods, including diamonds, antiques, art, tools, and other items that might be expected to retain some measure of their value.

Demand for oil, fuel, and many hard and soft commodities has also surged during periods of runaway inflation. More than likely, U.S.-based buying triggered by hyperinflation will set in motion the next leg of the long-term commodity supercycle that investors such as Jim Rogers and Marc Faber have long discussed, where prices ultimately trend higher for two or more decades. Over time, the hyperinflation will burn itself out, either because of a regime change in the United States or an abrupt return to fiscal sanity. By then, however, the world will appear a very dark place, with all hope seemingly lost. But if history is any guide, a welter of new opportunities will abound.

15

RELATIONSHIPS

"Trust, but verify."

—President Ronald Regan

More than a decade ago, John Lauer, a certified financial planner and director of risk management and benefits for the Chicago Housing Authority (CHA), was offered the chance to invest pension plan assets in a fund that would achieve lucrative returns by repeatedly buying and selling securities issued by prime banks. On its face, it seemed like good idea. Early retirements at the agency had led to a deficit in the CHA plan, and an investment that could generate double-digit gains would help fill the gap. Moreover, the strategy seemed to have a lot going for it aside from mouth-watering returns. Performance would be achieved through low-risk arbitrage in prime bank guarantees; the program would include only the top 25 European banks; funds would remain under the investor's control and could be withdrawn at any time; and other institutions, including a substantial trust, had already gotten involved.

Unfortunately for the Chicago Housing Authority, the "roll program," as it was known, was a complete sham. "Prime bank guarantees" did not—and do not—exist. The idea of compounding gains by repeatedly buying and selling securities was nothing more than smoke and mirrors. Invested funds of at least $12.5 million were quickly siphoned off in the form of "fees" to Mr. Lauer—one reason why, perhaps, *he* might have believed it was an investment worth pursuing—and ill-gotten gains to the various other participants, and the pension plan still had a deficit.

If history is any guide, the coming economic and financial meltdown will create an environment ripe for fraud, chicanery, and deception. Phrases such as *high yield, double-digit return, guaranteed,* and *low-risk,* spoken or written in close proximity to one another, will seem like manna from heaven to vulnerable individuals with bills to pay or sizable financial holes to fill. Yet more than ever, the admonition about being "too good to be true" will be too important to be ignored.

Whether stirred by pent-up greed or gullibility borne out of despair, many personal and professional relationships will be severely tested when the economy, the financial system, and the social fabric simultaneously unravel. Indeed, it will be difficult to predict how anyone—including family or friends; managers or partners; colleagues or employees; and leaders or fellow members of religious, fraternal, and social organizations—will react under such circumstances. In the past, at least, desperate people have sometimes resorted to desperate measures, like embezzling funds or stealing valuable items and selling them off.

Corruption will likely become endemic, especially as economic contraction devolves into a hyperinflationary spiral. Still, it won't just be bonds of honor and crimes of opportunity that Americans will have to worry about. Scammers, con artists, identity thieves, and a wide range of hard-core criminal types will also be inspired to step up the pace of their illegal activities. Painful economic conditions will not only leave Americans more exposed but will also lead to cutbacks in law enforcement, the legal system, and other government programs as well as private sector services, such as parking-lot security and emergency lighting, which make for a generally safer environment. Increasingly, the bad guys will be given free reign to do as they please.

Stoked by the one-two punch of collapsing demand and a growing systemic crisis, a rapid rise in bankruptcies in combination with an explosion of lawsuits and the likelihood of abrupt changes in government policies could also put people's financial well-being at risk.

During such times, the American sensibility, long characterized by trust and faith in others, will need to become more discriminating. Survival will necessitate caution and due diligence rather than openness and easy acceptance. It will be better to favor established enterprises over newer firms, large companies with considerable resources over businesses with little staying power, solid reputations over fancy offers, and plain talk over jargon. It will also be a time, as in those long-uttered admonishments to children, to beware of strangers. If gut instincts suggest that something does not seem quite right, Americans will need to stand back and learn more before committing.

A collapsing economy and deteriorating safety nets will lead to the widespread establishment of personal support networks populated with family and friends. No doubt, people will have to work closely with those in their inner circle, nurturing and strengthening these relationships for practical as well as emotional and other reasons. But at the same time, they must be on guard against the possibility that someone near and dear to them may blow a gasket and do the wrong thing. However paranoid it sounds, people will need to have enough information about those they depend on to minimize the danger of being victimized. This idea is not intended to advocate a Stalinist world built on mutual distrust. Rather, it is a question of being careful, because misjudgments about other people will leave much less room for error than before.

As noted earlier, knowledge and awareness will be an important source of strength in a world of chaos and insecurity. The long-established, though often omitted, practice of carefully checking references, probing inconsistencies, and only gradually becoming comfortable with new acquaintances and business relationships will provide a minimum standard of protection. Following an era defined by aggressive networking and persona-building, however, the benefits might be limited. But as large tracts of what were once private data become public, the Internet can increasingly enable the due diligence that should not only apply with respect to business and financial matters but to relationships of all sorts.

There are pitfalls in acquiring intelligence online, not the least of which is the amount of worthless, incorrect, and misleading information in circulation. Then there are the inherent difficulties of wading through large volumes of information. Even with the shortcomings, however, a basic Internet-based background check will potentially yield enough useful intelligence about individuals, employers, and advisors to act as an important first line of defense against what could be a dangerous ride. All sorts of public records, news items, opinions, rumors, social-networking connections, official relationship details, and other data can be found floating in the digital ocean.

Perhaps the easiest and best-known approach to gathering intelligence is to search Web sites such as *www.google.com, www.yahoo. com, www.msn.com,* and *www.ask.com,* each of which occasionally yields links that do not overlap with the others' results. Those services also offer options, whether accessible separately or as a built-in feature, to sift through current and archived news reports, journal-like sites known as blogs, digital images, and media files. In addition, some search services are targeted to a variety of special needs, particularly relating to people. For information on telephone numbers or addresses, for example, there are online versions of traditional telephone directories such as *www.superpages. com,* Verizon's version of the Yellow pages, along with digital-only offerings like *http://anywho.com, www.411.com,* and *http://infospace .com.* Services oriented towards collecting public information about individuals and intelligently collating the material are a variant of traditional search engines like Google. Among the most useful are *www.zoominfo.com* and *http://zabasearch.com.* Other specialized repositories can also be accessed on the Internet, including *http://birthdatabase.com,* which can reveal information about birth dates, and the Social Security Death Index, a database of deaths reported since 1962 to the Social Security Administration, accessible at *http://ssdi.rootsweb.com.*

Online newspaper and magazine articles and archives, such as those found at *http://nytimes.com, www.washingtonpost.com,* and *http://online.wsj.com* can be great places to uncover useful information. Comprehensive databases of articles and reports from newspapers, magazines, and other publications can also be searched for a fee at *http://factiva.com, www.lexisnexis.com,* and similar sites.

Aside from those resources, a great deal of public sector data is becoming available online, often at no cost, including real estate, civil and criminal court, licensing, tax, and other records. Three sites that detail where to find this information are *http:// publicrecordfinder.com, http://publicrecordcenter.com,* and *http://brbpub .com/pubrecsites.asp.* Although small fees are involved, federal court records can be accessed through the Public Access to Court Electronic Records system (PACER) found at *http://pacer.psc.uscourts .gov.* Online municipal court and other records, in contrast, can usually be found by exploring state and local government Web sites, a directory of which is at *http://statelocalgov.net.*

Virtually all of these intelligence-gathering methods will also prove useful for keeping tabs on employers, partners, vendors, landlords, customers, and any other parties that could affect one's financial future if the relationship turned sour. Certain relationships, like those with doctors, caregivers, teachers, and contractors, will be about more than just money. Extra precautions, such as checking with licensing or other authorities, whether or not the data are available online, should be taken as a matter of course.

With the economy in trouble, money tight, and the fallout from an exploding systemic crisis causing broad shockwaves, businesses will take aggressive and dramatic steps to contain the damage. These measures might include closing plants, slashing jobs, or filing for bankruptcy. It will be necessary to stay attuned to what is or might soon be happening rather than risk being blindsided. The effort will require, at a minimum, the same degree of due diligence needed to keep tabs on individual relationships, though with more persistent follow-up. The dynamic between employers and employees will undoubtedly skew in favor of the former as conditions deteriorate, with corporate survival turned into a blunt instrument to repel demands for better working conditions or higher compensation. Under such circumstances, loyalty will count for very little, and any sense of moral obligation to the longer-term welfare of workers will continue to erode.

Firms that are already in trouble or that depend on industries considered vulnerable will need to be monitored closely, especially if they represent a primary source of household income. That means keeping an eye open for any sort of hard news as well as opinions, rumors, and hearsay. Of particular importance will be information regarding creditworthiness and financial wherewithal. News that the company in question, a large rival, or a key supplier has had its credit rating cut or marked for a possible downgrade by any rating agency should be interpreted as a red flag requiring immediate attention.

Still, figuring out which firms will or won't survive at a time of unprecedented upheaval will be more of a crapshoot than ever. Even during the so-called normal years, some firms fell from grace unexpectedly and abruptly. At one time, for example, Enron was the seventh largest company in America, but as a result of massive fraud, the company evolved from blue-chip favorite to belly-up pariah in less than a year. And within 13 months of the 9/11 terrorist bombings, two airlines had filed for bankruptcy, while the rest of the industry racked up billions of dollars in losses.

With that in mind, most Americans will have little choice but to keep one ear to the ground. The Internet isn't the only research source, of course. Public libraries are a free and relatively underutilized access point for all kinds of valuable reference materials, directories, and specialized databases, though over time they will almost certainly face the same budgetary squeeze as other public sector services. Under the circumstances, much intelligence will need to come from the fast-expanding digital ocean.

Electronic editions of business newspapers like *http://online .wsj.com* (mentioned above), *www.ft.com*, and *http://bloomberg.com* as well as financial portals like *http://finance.yahoo.com, http:// money.cnn.com, http://marketwatch.com*, and *www.thestreet.com* will prove useful. Many of these sites, along with others sponsored by the likes of Google and Yahoo, allow users to create and subscribe to alerts, where stories mentioning selected keywords, such as the name of an employer, can be automatically tracked or transmitted by e-mail. Important searches can also be recalled in various ways, either by saving the link stemming from a query as a "favorite" in a Web browser such as Internet Explorer or by creating preprogrammed searches at sites that allow them to be stored for future use.

Sites with content specifically related to business or particular companies and industries may also be worthwhile locations to do some digital digging. Trade association Web sites can be good, though not necessarily unbiased, places to start, along with business information portals like *http://hoovers.com*. Other helpful resources include the Securities and Exchange Commission's Electronic Data Gathering, Analysis, and Retrieval system (EDGAR), accessible at *www.sec.gov/edgar/searchedgar/webusers.htm*.

The Web sites of government watchdogs like the Federal Trade Commission, at *http://ftc.gov*, as well as various state attorneys general and consumer protection agencies, occasionally provide information about individuals, firms, and industries that have run afoul of the law. Also deserving a mention are consumer protection Web sites, such as *http://consumeraction.gov, www.lookstoogood tobetrue.com, www.nclnet.org*, and *http://bbb.org*. At *www.epls.gov*, there is a list of individuals and firms that have had problems in their dealings with the U.S. government and have been excluded from receiving benefits from federal contracts.

Employing a thorough approach and following up as necessary will be essential. In a world quickly becoming unglued, a glowing past might not provide enough insight on what could happen tomorrow. In other words, complacent assumptions about relationships could lead to serious but unnecessary problems down the road.

These and other precautions will prove absolutely necessary when it comes to relationships with bankers, brokers, insurance agents, investment advisors, accountants, or other fiduciaries as well as with any other counterparties that could directly impact personal finances. Americans should stay on top of their ties with financial institutions in the same way that they themselves have been monitored in an era of regular electronic credit checks. A weak or falling credit rating for an insurer might mean it will be unable or even unwilling to make good on a claim after premiums have already been paid, while the failure of a broker, as with Refco, might cause funds to be tied up for months, potentially leading to a personal liquidity crisis.

The need for constant vigilance cannot be overstated. But the dangers won't stem only from traditional counterparty risks. Financial well-being could also be undercut by a blurring of the lines between principal and agency activities, an increased emphasis by many institutions and representatives on turnover and production at the expense of long-term fiduciary responsibility, and rules changes that boost the potential for conflicts of interest, such as the pension reform legislation enacted in 2006 that allows 401(k) plan administrators to offer advice to investors.

Combined, these factors make a strong case for diversification of financial relationships. Still, they represent a paradox. On the one hand, narrowing down the list of individuals or firms qualified to handle one's finances should be an important aspect of a personal protection strategy. On the other hand, there can be no guarantees about which relationships might eventually turn sour. Just as no small number of banks or brokers will be forced to shut their doors because of fraud, mismanagement, or the fallout from a burgeoning financial crisis, firms that engage in the safekeeping of personal valuables or precious metal investments could also close down abruptly or be affected by government confiscation.

When it comes to the number of points of contact with an organization, more will invariably be better than less. The risks of doing business with those that can only be reached online or via e-mail could be high, whether because of inopportune outages and technological hiccups or something more sinister. Many people may be surprised at the extent to which counterparty risks have become embedded in modern-day financial products, practices, and markets. In fact, the creditworthiness and liquidity charac-teristics of many money market funds, ETFs, MBSs, and munici-pal bonds are closely tied, in one way or another, to the fortunes of intermediaries, such as sponsors, guarantors, depositaries, and agents.

With that in mind, knowing as much as possible about any financial relationships will be an essential part of protecting in-vestments and assets from the coming perfect storm. In addition to the approaches and methods cited earlier, other resources are available online that can help Americans keep an eye on individu-als or firms that, in one way or another, deal with money-related matters.

Places to check include the Web sites of banking regulators such as the Federal Reserve, the Office of Thrift Supervision, the Federal Deposit Insurance Corporation, and the Office of the Comptroller of the Currency, at *http://federalreserve.gov, www.ots. treas.gov, www.fdic.gov*, and *www.occ.treas.gov*, respectively. The on-line access points of agencies that monitor investment banks, bro-kers, exchanges, and securities markets, including the Securities and Exchange Commission, the Commodities Futures Trading Commission, and the National Association of Securities Dealers, at *http://sec.gov, http://cftc.gov*, and *www.nasd.com*, respectively, also have much to offer. In addition, state securities administrators keep separate tabs on such activities that take place in their own jurisdictions. A directory of links to individual state Web sites is at *www.nasaa.org*.

Both the SEC and NASD maintain databases containing con-tact information, career history, regulatory backgrounds, current affiliations, and other pertinent details about individuals and firms that are authorized to engage in the securities business, including brokers and investment advisors. These can be accessed through links from their main sites. Although the banking and securities sectors are monitored by authorities at both the national and state level, the insurance industry is primarily overseen by state regulators. Links to the relevant Web sites for each of the agencies are listed at *http://naic.org*.

Apart from government overseers, virtually all financial institutions and many of their outstanding bonds and other securities are evaluated by private agencies. These include relatively well-known entities such as Standard & Poor's, Moody's, Fitch, and insurance sector specialist A.M. Best. It's worth keeping in mind, however, that they often receive requests for ratings from, and are paid by, the subject firms themselves, which can represent a potential conflict of interest. Several offer free data on ratings to the public as well as helpful alert features that notify subscribers of a change. Also, agencies such as Weiss Ratings, at *http://weissratings. com*, evaluate the financial condition of numerous banks, insurers, and other entities but don't take any compensation or direction from the firms they review. Listings of other independent rating services can be found at the FDIC and SEC Web sites.

With respect to certain key advisors, including lawyers and accountants, the best source of information tends to be state licensing agencies, though not all of them offer online access or respond to queries in a timely fashion. Bar associations and other professional and trade groups can also be of assistance, though these organizations have an inherent obligation to members that can be at odds with the needs of their clients.

While it clearly makes sense to mitigate the risks associated with myriad social, economic, and financial relationships, affiliating with certain large groups may offer advantages. Unions, as noted previously, will almost certainly gain in power and influence in response to deteriorating conditions and an unsustainable shift in the employer-worker dynamic. Getting involved with other groups whose members have common characteristics, philosophies, or goals may also yield benefits. The American Association of Retired Persons (AARP) provides information, stirs debate, and advocates legislation on behalf of older Americans. Of course, any organization could be at risk of being infiltrated by extremists or having its policies and programs directed away from the needs of the majority.

Minimizing the potential fallout from bad relationships may necessitate other steps, including keeping personal property secured under lock and key, implementing freezes or fraud alerts at credit bureaus to reduce the risk of identity theft, and favoring physical control of assets over receipts, book entries, and other indirect methods of ownership. Protecting one's interests might also mean placing assets clearly out of harm's way, safe from lawsuits, creditors, and breakups. That might entail separating personal affairs from business-related risks or using legitimate legal mechanisms such as trusts and offshore accounts to limit access, though it is best to check with an experienced, trustworthy advisor.

Finally, moving funds overseas, which will almost certainly be imperative as the American monetary system and social structure breaks down completely, involves risks in its own right, including the possibilities of political upheaval, war, changing financial regulations, the imposition of cross-border currency and capital controls, and corruption or other criminal activity. Avoiding these dangers will require even more due diligence. Still, no matter which phase of the unraveling is under way, the key will be to stay informed and remain alert—before it's too late.

16

LIFESTYLE

"Wealth consists not in having great possessions but in having few wants."
—Epicurus

When blogs—or "web logs," as they were originally called—began appearing in the early 1990s, they were unique digital outlets for personal expression. They were like online diaries, except that they were openly available for anyone to read. As they gained in popularity and sophistication, people began using them as a way to communicate ideas on a broad range of subjects, from technology and finance to culture and politics, and to collaborate with others from around the globe. Blogs even started overtaking traditional media outlets as a source of breaking news and real-time commentary in some cases, with blogging occasionally referred to as "citizen journalism."

In recent years, blogs have been one of the fastest-growing phenomena on the Internet, providing access to a broad array of insights and tips on virtually any topic, including consumer finance and personal investing. But the explosion in content has also made it difficult to track down or isolate information that is especially useful or relevant. Fortunately there are Web sites where digital material is screened by individuals with an active or even a passionate interest in the subject, and some technology-driven services sift through, sort, and collate the mountain of data.

At a time of economic and financial upheaval, traditional news and information channels will, more often than not, fixate on the economic wreckage and emotional fallout rather than planning ahead for more of the same. They will also be subject to censorship and bombarded with propaganda and wishful thinking by those who don't or won't see what is really going on.

Taken together, those crosscurrents will generate scads of distracting "noise" that will probably be of little value in coping with difficult, rapidly changing circumstances. More than ever, having ready access to critical, up-to-the-minute intelligence could be the difference between not surviving, just barely making it, or successfully swimming upstream when others are sinking fast. To rise above insecurity and doubt, as well as anxiety and fear, it will be necessary to remain alert to the cold, hard reality unfolding each day, no matter how unpalatable, and focus on being objective.

Once more, knowing where to find what is needed will be as important as having access to it. Fortunately, advances in technology will provide an entry point that did not exist before the era of the information superhighway. Indeed, by shrinking the gap between information haves and have-nots and enabling the rapid dissemination of vital intelligence, the Internet will allow ordinary Americans to keep abreast of what is going on to an unprecedented degree. Deciding which sites to monitor will of course depend on individual needs and interests, though some will have broad appeal.

Aside from those already mentioned, there are a plethora of choices, running the gamut from generalist consumer sites, such as *http://consumerist.com* and *www.consumerismcommentary.com*, to those that describe unusual but successful businesses that people have created, often out of necessity, such as *http://uncommon business.blogspot.com*. Another approach is to monitor sites that feature continuously updated links to a variety of blogs and sites offering insights on budgeting, saving, investment, and other key financial topics. One good example is *http://pfblogs.org*, which bills itself as the Ad-Free Personal Finance Blogs Aggregator.

Alternatively, people can stay on top of important developments by creating customized lists of blogs and the sites of other Web-based providers that "syndicate" their content using "feeds." RSS, Atom, and the variously named feeds are essentially reformatted versions of the same data available at the host location, standardized for easy distribution around the Internet. They can be viewed using programs called "feed readers" or the "aggregator" services found at *www.bloglines.com* and elsewhere. These applications enable users to peruse quickly or monitor efficiently content from a host of different providers. Many also allow users to be notified—by e-mail or special desktop software—if and when new content is posted.

Other services can also tap into what is known as the "blogosphere." Apart from blog-specific functions at Google and Yahoo, targeted search applications like those found at *www.feedster.com* and *http://technorati.com* can also sift through the specialized content, including very recent postings.

Just having access to information won't be all that matters. Attitudes and approaches will have to change as well. For most Americans, the period ahead will be a time to scrimp and scrape and shy away from a natural sense of optimism that says tomorrow will be better than today. Instead of looking for handouts or loans, people will increasingly have to draw upon their own creative inner spirit to satisfy whatever needs they might have and uncover alternatives to spending money, without necessarily expending a great deal of valuable time and energy in the process.

As noted earlier, the focus must be on eradicating debt and forgoing borrowing wherever possible. A lifestyle that depends on borrowed money or leverage in one form or another to meet unexpected shortfalls or to ratchet up resources will likely prove irresponsible and possibly lethal when the economy is in a downward spiral and household finances are increasingly under the gun. After years of ultimately unsustainable profligacy, Americans will have to disavow consumption habits driven by illusory affordability and the size of monthly payments. They must also become far more disciplined, learning how to say "No," "Later," or, "Let's think about this first," while also setting a solid example for those who are nearest and dearest.

Some will also have to come to terms with a long-nurtured addiction to spending for spending's sake as well as the modern-day view of shopping as entertainment. No doubt the pain of staying away from the call of the mall will mirror the withdrawal symptoms associated with quitting other bad habits cold turkey. Sticking to a routine of accumulating resources ahead of seemingly endless rainy days might seem dreary, but the alternative will surely be worse. Saving doesn't just mean stashing away whatever is left over after the spending is done, however; squirreling away funds should be treated as an unavoidable expense in its own right.

Many seemingly alien concepts of the past, such as living frugally, conserving and recycling, and cutting back on nonessentials, will have to be recast from a 21st-century perspective. That might mean eliminating unwatched cable TV channels, making coffee at home rather than going to Starbucks, or reading a library book instead of renting a DVD—and more than likely, a whole lot more. The new reality will force Americans to pay close attention to what they need and what is truly important in an economic sense and, perhaps, a spiritual sense. Money woes will invariably invite a host of other difficulties, including stress and conflict, suffering and sadness, and depression and illness.

If that happens, family and spiritual bonds, as well as an appreciation for the simpler things in life, will have to fill a void for which money or gratuitous consumption was once a crude substitute. Perhaps the economic unraveling presents an opportunity to rediscover values that once mattered a great deal to many Americans.

To be sure, addressing the financial situation will remain paramount when the wheels are falling off the economic wagon. Querying everything and anything having to do with earning, spending, saving, and even borrowing must be a relentless concern. Individuals and families will need to formulate realistic and sensible answers to questions like, "Do we really need two cars—or even one at all?" "Are our current accommodations too large?" "Can we get more use out of aging appliances and other household items?" and "Must we have the latest gadgets?"

There will be little to gain and much to lose by cutting back on critical maintenance expenditures, however; doing so costs more in the long run, either because replacements are needed sooner than expected or because of needless accidents. Experience suggests, for example, that automobiles remain roadworthy for longer when the engine oil is changed regularly, while regular servicing of costly home heating and cooling systems can extend their useful lives.

Spending on food and other household necessities should also be analyzed under a microscope. Rather than buying heavily marketed brands or those that have been used mainly out of habit, it might make more sense to favor cheaper, no-name alternatives. And instead of buying takeout or highly processed, elaborately packaged food, which tends to cost more than the homemade variety, Americans should consider using healthier, fresher ingredients that can be prepared the old-fashioned way. Products that are readily available and can be sourced locally will likely prove to be the best choice in the long run, as worsening economic conditions and growing trade wars lead to shortages, long lines, and price hikes for some staples.

Consuming ingredients that are more wholesome and natural will also be healthier. In fact, taking steps to improve physical well-being will likely be a necessity for many Americans, as the quality, availability, and affordability of private and public health care diminishes and a working "retirement" becomes an unavoidable reality. It goes without saying that eliminating such bad habits as smoking will offer numerous benefits. Certainly when times are hard, it will be difficult to rein in activities that, for some people at least, help to alleviate stress or act as an escape. Practically speaking, though, people will have to think of alternatives that are less physically and financially taxing, such as regular exercise or even meditation.

With the prospect of regular shortages and blackouts as well as higher prices, energy consumption in all its forms should be addressed as well. Some basic steps might include walking instead of driving; turning off appliances, heaters, air conditioners, and other devices not in use; layering clothing or adjusting thermostats; and evaluating alternative energy sources based on longer-run economic considerations.

Some expenses cannot be avoided. The right approach to these will depend on which stage of the disaster is under way. When economic activity and prices are dropping sharply, waiting until the last possible moment before committing to any purchases will be the best strategy. Generally speaking, whatever something costs today will be less in future. In that case, adopting a kind of shopping siege mentality makes sense. That means engaging in comprehensive information gathering beforehand and looking for opportunities to haggle, renegotiate, or shop around, even for services like medical care, where driving a hard bargain is not an approach that is familiar to most Americans.

People must also be willing to substitute goods and services or even walk away from a prospective purchase if the terms aren't right. Other useful strategies will include cherry-picking products sold as loss leaders, hunting down coupons or unpublicized discounts, shopping at stores that benefit from high turnover, and timing purchases to take advantage of seasonal and retail cycles, including those motivated by monthly and quarterly sales quotas. Cutting back on the frequency of regular purchases, such as haircuts or dry cleaning, may also yield significant savings.

It will be an altogether different story when the monetary presses are running flat out and hyperinflation rages. Under those circumstances, shopping around and waiting to buy are absolutely the wrong things to do. In no time at all, in fact, this strategy could lead to impoverishment. Instead, cash should be spent as quickly as possible on necessities that will either be more expensive or unavailable tomorrow, or on tangible items whose values will tend to rise in line with the overall rate of inflation. More so than when prices are falling, Americans must stay attuned to prospective needs to avoid being forced to act out of desperation. One strategy that can pay significant dividends during a time of runaway inflation is to commit to purchases today that allow for preset payments to be made at a later date. Similarly useful are forward-purchase arrangements based on current prices, though the risk that the other side to the transaction may not honor its commitments certainly needs to be taken into account.

Strategies geared towards generating extra income shouldn't be left out of the equation, especially during the initial phase of what lies ahead. That might entail selling unwanted or unused items at online auction sites such as *www.ebay.com* or electronic marketplaces like *http://craigslist.org*. The key in both instances will be to do it as soon as possible, before everyone else is trying to do the same. Other revenue-generating options, including moonlighting at a second job or starting a home-based business that requires little in the way of overhead, should also be seriously considered.

Together, cutting expenses and boosting income will be the primary means of escape from the financial calamities that lie ahead, though Americans will also need to ensure that they are protected from other dangers. That means taking time to assess vulnerabilities, anticipating the cost of what can and will go wrong in future, and putting protective measures in place to mitigate the consequences.

No doubt, the fallout from a collapsing economy will foster all kinds of dangerous human-made risks, including those stemming from crimes against people and property, negligence and carelessness, and breakdowns in various public and private sector services and safety nets. However, certain locations, activities, and structures will be more at risk than will others. Inner cities and the large suburban areas that surround them will almost certainly see crime rates rise sharply in a dramatic turnabout from the relative quietude of recent years. The tentacles of the illegal drug trade will likely extend throughout society.

Under the circumstances, guarding against potentially violent individuals and other threats will be more important than ever, especially those that could victimize children and vulnerable adults. It will be time to emphasize personal safety, to lock doors and windows, and to put security measures in place that can protect life and property. Whether walking a short distance from home or through an unfamiliar neighborhood, eyes and ears should remain alert to signs of trouble. Common sense would also suggest that conspicuous consumption and ostentatious displays of wealth should be avoided.

Having the most appropriate forms and correct amounts of auto, life, and health insurance in place, as well as home and contents insurance to mitigate the risk of catastrophic loss, will be essential. Coverage decisions should be weighed against the prospect of having claims lowballed or arbitrarily rejected when the insurance company's financial condition worsens. Regardless, taking photos of insured property; maintaining comprehensive inventory lists; and keeping policies, receipts, valuations, and other documentation in a safe place may address those concerns.

Terrorist activities will go hand in hand with border disputes, political uprisings, unholy alliances, nationalization and confiscation, and other international threats as economic conditions worsen and the social mood sours. Personal disaster planning will therefore be imperative. Roads, tunnels, bridges, and other infrastructure facilities will be at greater risk of failing because of poor maintenance. In addition, financial markets, ATMs, payment systems, and various banking networks will likely face serious disruption because of systemic crises. Other developments, such as localized famines, environmental accidents, or even the growing prospect of pandemics may prove too much for the public or private sector to handle when budgets are slashed and resources are stretched to the limit. So will natural disasters, which are unlikely to see even the inadequate level of response that followed Hurricane Katrina.

Finally, when social and geopolitical conditions have deteriorated sufficiently, there will be other, potentially more pernicious threats. More than likely, Americans will be confronted by an unfamiliar and frightening array of legal, financial, and security restrictions, including lockdowns, curfews, internments, capital and exchange controls, and even martial law. Those who wish to survive the coming financial Armageddon will have little choice but to adjust as soon as possible to a world far removed from days gone by.

"A Brief History of Deposit Insurance in the United States," Prepared by various FDIC staff for the International Conference on Deposit Insurance, Washington, D.C., September 1998. *www.fdic.gov/bank/historical/brief/brhist.pdf* (accessed October 19, 2006).

"A World Awash with Profits." *The Economist,* February 12, 2005.

Abelson, Alan. "Call to ARMS: Anyone Know a Good Lawyer?" *Barron's,* June 26, 2006.

"ACLU Suggests U.S. May Be Spying on Three Other Financial Services," *The Raw Story,* July 19, 2006. *www.rawstory.com/ news/2006/ACLU_suggests_US_may_be_spying_0719.html* (accessed October 19, 2006).

Agence France-Presse. "Kissinger Warns of Possible 'War of Civilizations'." September 13, 2006.

Agence France-Presse. "U.S. Debt Clock Running Out of Time, Space." March 28, 2006.

Agence France-Presse. "U.S. Government Investigating Over 100 Companies in Stock Options Probe." September 6, 2006.

"Alan Greenspan: Monetary Myopia." *The Economist,* January 12, 2006.

Altman, Daniel. "Uncle Sam, Deadbeat Debtor?" *New York Times,* July 23, 2006.

Amato, Jeffrey D. "The International Debt Securities Market." *BIS Quarterly Review,* March 2006.

Anderson, Jenny. "As Lenders, Hedge Funds Draw Insider Scrutiny." *New York Times,* October 16, 2006.

Associated Press, "Higher Living Costs Prevent Retirement Savings: Survey Shows Americans Squeezed, but Know They Need to Save More." May 11, 2006.

Associated Press. "Medicare Seen Exhausting Reserves in Just 12 Years, Trustees Report." May 1, 2006.

Associated Press. "New Credit Card Minimums May Hurt Banks." March 12, 2006.

Associated Press. "Personal Bankruptcy Filings up 30 Percent Last Year, Hitting a High." March 26, 2006.

Associated Press. "U.S. Life Expectancy Rate Rises." December 8, 2005.

Atkins, Ralph, and Chris Giles. "ECB Warns of Hedge Funds' Threat to Stability." *FT.com*, June 2, 2006. *www.ft.com/cms/ s/112d2f36-f1d4-11da-940b-0000779e2340.html.* (accessed October 19, 2006).

Aversa, Jeannine, Associated Press. "Bernanke: Baby Boomers Will Strain U.S." October 4, 2006.

"Baby Boom and Bust: Will Share Prices Crash as Baby Boomers Sell Their Assets to Pay for Retirement?" *The Economist*, May 11, 2006.

Bajaj, Vikas. "Mortgages Grow Riskier, and Investors Are Attracted." *New York Times*, September 6, 2006.

Bajaj, Vikas, and Ron Nixon. "Re-refinancing and Putting Off Mortgage Pain," *New York Times.* July 23, 2006.

Baker, Dean. "The Menace of an Unchecked Housing Bubble," *Center for Economic and Policy Research.* March 16, 2006. *www.cepr.net/columns/baker/2006_03_30.htm* (accessed October 19, 2006).

Barcelo, Yan. "Vanilla or Rocky Road?" *CA Magazine*, March 1, 2006.

Barr, Stephen. "Retirement Fund Tapped to Avoid National Debt Limit." *Washington Post.* March 8, 2006.

Barr, Alistair. "Fannie Mae Could Be Hit Hard by Housing Bust: Berg. Mortgage Giant, Could Lose $29 billion, Long-Term Bear Argues in Investor Letter." *MarketWatch.com.* September 18, 2006. *www.marketwatch.com/News/Story/Story.aspx?guid=%7B843C8E17-B688-452B-96A8-524381ACC223%7D* (accessed October 19, 2006).

————. "Housing Slowdown Creating 'Ghost Towns.'" *MarketWatch.com.* October 16, 2006. *www.marketwatch.com/News/Story/5nXS5hK3Lhb0q4W6dK4T8DN?siteid=google&dist=TNMKTW* (accessed October 19, 2006).

Barrett, Emily. "Credit-Protection Industry Has Been Thriving. Expansion in Derivatives Fuels Concern over Risks. Downgrade for Thai Debt?" *Wall Street Journal,* September 20, 2006.

Barrett, Emily, and Madeleine Lim. "Credit-Derivatives Backlog Is Cut. Industry Has Cleared 70% of Unconfirmed Trades Outstanding, Fed Arm Says," *Wall Street Journal.* September 28, 2006.

Baum, Caroline. Bloomberg. "Slowdown Forecasters Are Living on Lonely Planet." May 3, 2006.

————. Bloomberg. "Banks Have No Exposure to Mortgages? Think Again." April 17, 2006.

Beales, Richard. "Boom Time for Derivatives Markets: Volumes Soar, but the Industry Is Under Pressure to Cut Backlogs and Increase Automation." *Financial Times* (London), March 16, 2006.

Beckner, Steven K. "Goldman's Corrigan: Final Shocks Less Likely but Could Be Worse." *Market News International,* May 17, 2006. *www.marketnews.com*

———. "U.S. Treasury's Henry: Must Get Arms Around Hedge Funds' Systemic Risk." *Market News International,* April 18, 2006. *www.marketnews.com*

Beck, Rachel, Associated Press. "Buyout Firms Are Saddling Debt on Ailing Companies." August 21, 2006.

Bruno, Joe Bel, Associated Press. "Former Fed Chair Alan Greenspan Says Housing Boom Over and Consumer Spending Could Taper." May 19, 2006.

Belt, Bradley D. Testimony of the executive director of the Pension Benefit Guaranty Corporation before the Committee on Budget, United States Senate. June 15, 2005. *www.dol .gov/ebsa/pdf/ty061505.pdf* (accessed October 19, 2006).

Bennett, Jessica. "Plastic Predicament: Credit Card Debt Has Nearly Tripled in the Last Two Decades, Leaving Many Americans Stuck in a Sinkhole of Fees and Penalties. Who's to Blame, Irresponsible Spenders or Predatory Lenders?" *Newsweek,* August 16, 2006. *www.msnbc.msn.com/id/14366431/ site/newsweek* (accessed October 19, 2006).

Berman, Dennis K. "Fistfuls of Dollars Fuel the M&A Engine." *Wall Street Journal,* January 3, 2006.

Bernanke, Ben S. "Hedge Funds and Systemic Risk." Remarks of the chairman of the Federal Reserve Board at the Federal Reserve Bank of Atlanta's 2006 Financial Market Conference, Sea Island, GA. May 16, 2006. *www.federalreserve.gov/ Boarddocs/speeches/2006/200605162/default.htm* (accessed October 19, 2006).

Bernstein, Aaron. "A Boomer Bust? Will Stock and Bond Markets Collapse as Retiring Baby Boomers Start Liquidating Assets? Two Experts Discuss the Question." *BusinessWeek*, April 26, 2006.

Bies, Susan Schmidt. "The Continuous Challenges of Risk Management." Remarks by the Federal Reserve Board governor at the Financial Services Institute, Washington, D.C., February 2, 2006. *www.federalreserve.gov/Boarddocs/speeches/2006/20060202/default.htm* (accessed October 19, 2006).

———. "A Risk Management Perspective on Recent Regulatory Proposals." Remarks by the Federal Reserve Board governor at America's Community Bankers Risk Management and Finance Forum, Naples, Florida, April 10, 2006. *www.federalreserve.gov/Boarddocs/speeches/2006/200604102/default.htm* (accessed October 19, 2006).

Birnbaum, Jeffrey H., and Chris Cillizza. "'Mortgage Moms May Star in Midterm Vote." *Washington Post*, September 5, 2006.

Blumenthal, Robin Goldwyn. "The Big Glut." *Barron's*, May 29, 2006.

Blustein, Paul. "Fissures Deep and Wide Shatter World Trade Talks." *Seattle Times*, July 5, 2006.

Borio, Claudio. "Market Distress and Vanishing Liquidity: Anatomy and Policy Options." Working Paper 158, Monetary and Economic Department, Bank for International Settlements, July 2004. *www.bis.org/publ/work158.pdf* (accessed October 19, 2006).

Borrus, Amy, Mike McNamee, and Howard Gleckman. "Uncle Sam: Up to His Neck in the Risk Pool." *BusinessWeek*, June 6, 2006.

Box, Steven. *Recession, Crime and Punishment.* London: Palgrave Macmillan, 1977.

Bradsher, Keith, and David Barboza. "Pollution from Chinese Coal Casts a Global Shadow." *New York Times,* June 11, 2006.

Braga, Michael. "Rental Market Caught in Real Estate Downturn." *Sarasota (FL) Herald Tribune,* August 7, 2006.

Brimelow, Peter. "On Watch for the Next LTCM." *MarketWatch,* May 11, 2006. *www.marketwatch.com/News/Story/Story. aspx?guid=%7BDA520BF5-1170-4CF0-8381-8EEF45655B05%7 D&siteid=mktw&dist* (accessed October 19, 2006).

Broaddus, Jr., J. Alfred. "Competition in Banking: Achieving the Right Balance." Speech of the past president of the Federal Reserve Bank of Richmond before the Bank Structure Conference, sponsored by the Federal Reserve Bank of Chicago, Chicago, Illinois, May 6, 2004. *www.richmondfed.org/ news_and_speeches/past_presidents_speeches/index.cfm/id=60* (accessed October 19, 2006).

Browning, E. S., and Justin Lahart. "Is Easy Money Going Down the Drain? Anxious Markets Closely Watch Push by World's Central Banks to Cut Off a Speculative Binge." *Wall Street Journal,* June 5, 2006.

Bucks, Brian K., Arthur B. Kennickell, and Kevin B. Moore, "Recent Changes in U.S. Family Finances: Evidence from the 2001 and 2004 Survey of Consumer Finances." *Federal Reserve Bulletin* 92 (February 2006).

Bucks, Brian K., and Karen Pence. "Do Homeowners Know Their House Values and Mortgage Terms?" Paper for the Federal Reserve Board of Governors. January 2006. *www.federalreserve .gov/Pubs/FEDS/2006/200603/200603pap.pdf* (accessed October 19, 2006).

Buffett, Warren E. "Chairman's Letter to Shareholders." Berkshire Hathaway, Inc. 2002 Annual Report.

————. "Chairman's Letter to Shareholders." Berkshire Hathaway, Inc. 2005 Annual Report.

Bull, Alister. Reuters. "Hedge Funds in View as Fed Ponders Systemic Risk." April 18, 2006.

Burnett, Tom. "Why Risk Is Rising for LBOs." *Barron's*, September 25, 2006.

Burns, Scott. "Total of Our Unfunded Liabilities Is Staggering: Social Security, Medicare Debt Huge Compared with U.S. Deficit." *Houston (TX) Chronicle*, May 14, 2006.

Burr, Barry B. "'Prime' Investment Scam Growing, SEC Says." *Pensions and Investments*, June 27, 1994.

Byron, Christopher. "Pension Powder: Underfunded Systems Set Stage for a Boomer Crisis." *New York Post*, November 7, 2005.

Cauchon, Dennis. "Retiree Benefits Grow into 'Monster.'" *USA Today*, May 24, 2006.

————. "What's the Real Federal Deficit?" *USA Today*, August 2, 2006.

Chittum, Ryan. "Commercial Real-Estate Peak Seen: Survey Expects '07 Pullback With Return of the Sector to Norm of Income Producer." *Wall Street Journal*, October 18, 2006.

Christie, Les. "The 'Danger Years' For Homeowners." *CNNMoney. com*, March 28, 2006. *http://money.cnn.com/2006/03/28/real_ estate/mortgage_danger_years/index.htm* (accessed October 19, 2006).

————. "Sharp Home Price Pullback: Government Index Shows the Largest Quarter-to-Quarter Falloff in Home Price Increases in Three Decades." *CNNMoney.com*, September 5, 2006. *http://money.cnn.com/2006/09/05/real_estate/Ofheo_home_prices/index.htm* (accessed October 19, 2006).

Clayton, Jonathan. "A Nation of Millionaires Who Can't Afford to Buy Anything." *Times* (London), May 8, 2006. *www.timesonline.co.uk/article/0,,3-2170099,00.html* (accessed October 19, 2006).

Clements, Jonathan. "The Debt Bubble Threatens to Derail Many Baby Boomers' Retirement Plans." *Wall Street Journal*, March 8, 2006.

Cohen, Norma. Ú.S. Pensions Body Warns Risk of Loss Has Risen Steeply." *Financial Times* (London), November 15, 2005.

Colvin, Geoffrey. "The End of a Dream: As Competitive Pressure Mounts, Even Healthy Firms Are Killing Off Pension Plans." *Fortune*, June 22, 2006.

Conkey, Christopher. "Typical U.S. Family's Net Worth Edged Up Only 1.5% in '01–'04." *Wall Street Journal*, February 24, 2006.

————. "Economy Leaps, but Wages Stagnate." *Wall Street Journal*, April 29, 2006.

Coombes, Andrea. "Home Is Where the Fraud Is: Mortgage Scams Cost Lenders Billions; Borrowers Hit, Too." MarketWatch.com, April 9, 2006. *www.marketwatch.com/News/Story/Story.aspx?guid=%7BF95A07EE-9C67-405F-8688-9542865B95B6%7D&dist=newsfinder&siteid=google&keyword=* (accessed October 19, 2006).

Cooper, Jim. "A Truer Measure of America's Ballooning Deficit." *Financial Times* (London), May 1, 2006.

Costo, Stephanie L. "Trends in Retirement Plan Coverage over the Last Decade." *Monthly Labor Review* 129, no. 2 (2006).

"Credit Derivatives Are Skewing Signals from the Bond Market." *Wall Street Journal Online,* May 15, 2006. *http://online.wsj.com/ PA2VJBNA4R/article/SB114765609864352610-search.html? KEYWORDS=credit+derivatives+skewing &COLLECTION=wsjie/ 6month* (accessed October 19, 2006).

Crenshaw, Albert B. "Match-Making for Savers." *Washington Post,* May 15, 2006.

Crutsinger, Martin, Associated Press. "Administration Says It Has Now Taken All Legal Actions to Avoid Hitting Debt Limit." March 6, 2006.

Cruz-Taura, Ana. "Soaring Insurance Costs Make Housing Less Affordable." Federal Reserve Bank of Atlanta's *Partners in Community and Economic Development* 16, no. 2 (2006).

CSU Newsline. "Study Puts Japanese Perceptions of California Rice to the Test." February 12, 2003. *www.calstate.edu/ Newsline/Archive/02-03/030212-Sac.shtml* (accessed October 19, 2006).

"Danger—Explosive Loans." *BusinessWeek,* October 23, 2006.

"The Dark Side of Debt: Public Markets for Raising and Investing Capital Are Plunging into the Shadows." *The Economist,* September 21, 2006.

Davies, Paul J. "Deutsche Could Be Tip of Iceberg." *Financial Times* (London), January 11, 2006.

Day, Kathleen. "Study Finds 'Extensive' Fraud at Fannie Mae: Bonuses Allegedly Drove the Scheme." *Washington Post,* May 24, 2006.

de Bono, Edward. *New Think: The Use of Lateral Thinking in the Generation of New Ideas.* New York: Basic Books, 1968.

de Rato, Rodrigo. Remarks of the managing director of the International Monetary Fund to the Frankfurt European Banking Congress, Frankfurt, Germany, November 18, 2005. *www.imf.org/external/np/speeches/2005/111805.htm* (accessed October 19, 2006).

Deener, Will. "Risks of Recession Continuing to Rise: Economy Is Slowing, Showing Warning Flags." *Chicago Tribune*, October 9, 2006.

DeLong, Brad. "The Odds of Economic Meltdown: With Interest Rates and Oil Prices Rising and Consumers Spending Beyond Their Means, We May Be Headed for Recession—and Worse." *Salon.com*, August 3, 2006. *www.salon.com/opinion/feature/2006/08/03/recession/index.html* (accessed October 19, 2006).

Delasantellis, Julian. "U.S. Living on Borrowed Time—and Money." *Asia Times Online*, March 24 2006. *www.atimes.com/atimes/Global_Economy/HC24Dj01.html* (accessed October 19, 2006).

Der Hovanesian, Mara. "Mortgage Lenders: Who's Most at Risk. As Delinquency Rates Rise, Red Flags Are Flying over Some Aggressive Finance Outfits." *BusinessWeek*, April 24, 2006.

———. "Nightmare Mortgages: They Promise the American Dream, a Home of Your Own—with Ultra-Low Rates and Payments Anyone Can Afford. Now, the Trap Has Sprung." *BusinessWeek*, September 11, 2006.

Der Hovanesian, Mara, and Dawn Kopecki. "Bad Blood over Bad Loans." *BusinessWeek*, October 2, 2006.

Derus, Michele. "Mortgage Fraud Growing Rapidly, Agencies Say." *Milwaukee Journal Sentinel*, May 15, 2006.

DiMartino, Danielle. "Fed Chief's Mercy May Have Costs." *Dallas Morning News,* January 30, 2006.

———. "Systemic Risk Is on the Bubble." *Dallas Morning News,* March 27, 2006.

DiStefano, Joseph N. "Don't Look for National Insurance Regulation Anytime Soon. Call It a Turf War. Or Call It Looking Out for the Little Guy. Even Consumer Advocates Favor the Status Quo." *Philadelphia Enquirer,* July 17, 2005.

"The Dogs of Debt Shall Bark: The Corporate Bond Market Is Riskier Than It Looks." *Economist.com,* September 12, 2006. *www.economist.com/research/articlesBySubject/displayStory.cfm? story_id=7903581&subjectid=2512631* (accessed October 19, 2006).

Donlan, Thomas G. "Delusions of Adequacy: How the Federal Government Reviews the Performance of Its Programs." *Barron's,* March 6, 2006.

———. "Indebted to Debt: Credit Cards Smooth Out the Rough Spots in the Economy," *Barron's,* December 5, 2005.

———. "No Laughing Matter: The Social Security and Medicare Reports Are Absurd, but Not Funny." *Barron's,* May 8, 2006.

Donmoyer, Ryan J. Bloomberg. "Walker Says Wall Street 'Missing in Action' on Debt." March 17, 2006.

Cameron, Doug, and Krishna Guha. "Bernanke Tells Banks to Be Vigilant on Home Loans." *Financial Times* (London), May 19, 2006.

Downey, Kirstin. "Doors Close for Real Estate Speculators." *Washington Post,* April 22, 2006.

Dreazen, Yochi J. "Russia-U.S. Shift in Power Balance May Mold Summit." *Wall Street Journal,* July 10, 2006.

Dubow, Charles. "Foreclosures: Down, but Not Much Longer. The Good News Is That Foreclosures Were Down in the Second Quarter. The Bad News: They Will Get Worse by the End of the Year." *BusinessWeek Online*, August 10, 2006. *www.businessweek.com/investor/content/aug2006/pi20060810_284614.htm* (accessed October 19, 2006).

Dugan, John C. Remarks of the comptroller of the currency before the Consumer Federation of America, December 1, 2005. *www.occ.treas.gov/ftp/release/2005-117a.pdf* (accessed October 19, 2006).

Durfee, Don, and Sara Johnson. "CFOs' Optimism at 5-Year Low." *CFO.com*, September 13, 2006. *www.cfo.com/article .cfm/7905209* (accessed October 19, 2006).

"East Asian Economies Must Prepare for Possible Sharp US Dollar Slide-ADB." *AFX News Limited*, March 28, 2006. *www .forbes.com/business/feeds/afx/2006/03/28/afx2625991.html* (accessed October 19, 2006).

Eckholm, Erik. "America's 'Near Poor' Are Increasingly at Economic Risk, Experts Say." *New York Times*, May 8, 2006.

"Elliott Waves and Social Reality." *Socionomics Institute. www .socionomics.net/social_reality.html* (accessed October 19, 2006).

Eisinger, Jesse. "Debt Party: Investors Scoff at Risk, but Their Borrowing May Haunt Them." *Wall Street Journal*, March 22, 2006.

———. "Debt-Laden Consumers Present Problems for Economy." *Wall Street Journal*, January 4, 2006.

———. "Mortgage Market Begins to See Cracks as Subprime Loan Problems Emerge." *Wall Street Journal*, August 30, 2006.

Ely, Bert. "The Federal Financial Sector Safety Net: An Overview of the Issues." Financial Services Roundtable, March 2001. *www.fsround.org/PDFs/elypaper.PDF+bert+ely+financial+services+roundtable+safety+net&hl=en&gl=us&ct=clnk&cd=1* (accessed October 19, 2006).

Evans-Pritchard, Ambrose. "Monday View: Why Break-Up of Faltering Euro Could Be the Way Ahead." *Daily Telegraph* (London), September 18, 2006.

"Fannie and Freddie at Risk, Treasury Says." *Seattle (WA) Times,* June 27, 2006.

"The Fannie Exception." *Wall Street Journal,* May 10, 2006.

"Fannie Mae's Spiraling Troubles." *Wall Street Journal Online,* May 9, 2006. *http://online.wsj.com/PA2VJBNA4R/article/SB114718804359347827-search.html?KEYWORDS=fannie+mae%27s+spiraling & COLLECTION=wsjie/6month* (accessed October 19, 2006).

Farrell, Paul B. "Tipping Point Pops Bubble, Triggers Bear: Ten Warnings the Economy, Markets Have Pushed into Danger Zone." *MarketWatch,* August 21, 2006. *www.marketwatch.com/news/story/story.aspx?guid=%7B9FE7F780-DF3B-46FA-BB3D-5104309EEEA5%7D* (accessed October 19, 2006).

"Federal Lending Programs," *Center on Federal Financial Institutions, www.coffi.org/lending_progs.html.*

Feisst, Melanie. "Hedge Funds Storm to $1.5 Trillion." *Daily Telegraph* (London), March 16, 2006.

Ferguson, Jr., Roger W. "The Future of Financial Services—Revisited." Remarks of the vice chairman of the Federal Reserve Board at the Future of Financial Services Conference, Boston, Massachusetts, October 8, 2003. *www.federalreserve.gov/boarddocs/speeches/2003/200310082/default.htm* (accessed October 19, 2006).

"Financial Stability Forum Worried by High Household Debt, House Prices." *AFX News Limited,* September 6, 2006. *www.forbes.com/markets/feeds/afx/2006/09/06/afx2997462.html* (accessed October 19, 2006).

Fisher, Daniel. "A Dangerous Game: Hedge Funds Have Gotten Rich from Credit Derivatives. Will They Blow Up?" *Forbes,* October 16, 2006.

Fleckenstein, Bill. "Voodoo Debt and the Coming Recession: With Debt Piled High in a Variety of Voodoo Mortgages, the Declining Economy Will Soon Turn into a Bobsled Ride to Tears." *MSN Money,* September 25, 2006. *http:// articles.moneycentral.msn.com/Investing/ContrarianChronicles/ VoodooDebtAndTheComingRecession.aspx* (accessed October 19, 2006).

Flikerski, Amy. "Learning from History: It Is Said Those Who Don't Learn from History Are Doomed to Repeat It. The Markets Are Littered with Carcasses of Those Who Didn't Heed This Warning." Derived from a speech by Highbridge Capital's Henry Swieca, "Here Are Some Case Studies of Market Shocks and Panics and What Traders Should Learn," *Futures,* October 1, 2005.

"Foreclosures Up 72 Percent from Last Year," RealtyTrac™ U.S. Foreclosure Market Report (First Quarter, 2006). *www.realtytrac.com/pub/articles/aol/foreclosure_trends_2006Q1 .asp?m=1* (accessed October 19, 2006).

Frankel, Allen. "Prime or Not So Prime? An Exploration of U.S. Housing Finance in the New Century." *BIS Quarterly Review,* March 2006.

Freudenheim, Milt, and Mary Williams Walsh. "The Next Retirement Time Bomb." *New York Times,* December 11, 2005.

Galbraith, John Kenneth. "The 1929 Parallel." *Atlantic Online*, January 1987. *www.theatlantic.com/doc/198701/galbraith* (accessed October 19, 2006).

Gangahar, Anuj. "Why Volatility Is a New Asset Class." *Financial Times* (London), May 24, 2006.

"GDP Growth: With and Without Mortgage Extraction." Calculated Risk, December 9, 2005 blog entry. *http:// calculatedrisk.blogspot.com/2005/12/gdp-growth-with-and-without-mortgage.html* (accessed October 19, 2006).

Geithner, Timothy F. "Hedge Funds and Derivatives and Their Implications for the Financial System." Remarks by the president and chief executive officer of the Federal Reserve Bank of New York at the Distinguished Lecture 2006, sponsored by the Hong Kong Monetary Authority and Hong Kong Association of Banks, Hong Kong, September 15, 2006. *www.ny.frb.org/newsevents/speeches/2006/gei060914.html* (accessed October 19, 2006).

————. "Risk Management Challenges in the U.S. Financial System." Remarks by the president and chief executive officer of the Federal Reserve Bank of New York at the Global Association of Risk Professionals 7th Annual Risk Management Convention and Exhibition, New York, February 28, 2006. *www.newyorkfed.org/newsevents/ speeches/2006/gei060228.html* (accessed October 19, 2006).

"General Motors, Delphi, and the Unions: Last Tango in Detroit?" *The Economist*, April 6, 2006.

Gerena-Morales, Rafael. "Across U.S., Rising Property Taxes Spark Revolts. Activists in 20 States Push Legislation, Citizen Ballots, or Lawsuits to Gain Relief." *Wall Street Journal*, February 1, 2006.

Gimein, Mark. "Is a Hedge Fund Shakeout Coming Soon? This Insider Thinks So." *New York Times*, September 4, 2006.

Gladwell, Malcolm. *The Tipping Point: How Little Things Can Make a Big Difference.* New York: Little, Brown and Company, 2000.

"Global House Prices: Soft Isn't Safe." *The Economist,* March 2, 2006.

Glover, John. Bloomberg. "Accounting Errors in Asset-Backed Debt Are Rising." April 20, 2006.

Gogoi, Pallavi. "The Real Problem with Job Growth: U.S. Retailers Are No Longer the Job-Creation Engine They Were, Suggesting That Consumers May Finally Be Crying 'Uncle'." *BusinessWeek,* July 12, 2006.

"Goldman Sachs: On Top of the World. In Its Taste for Risk, the World's Leading Investment Bank Epitomizes the Modern Financial System." *The Economist,* April 27, 2006.

Gongloff, Mark. "Fearing a Fed Fallout." *Wall Street Journal Online,* April 7, 2006. *http://online.wsj.com/ PA2VJBNA4R/article/SB114435720873919209-search.html? KEYWORDS=fearing+a+fed+fallout&COLLECTION=wsjie/6mont* (accessed October 19, 2006).

Grant, James. "Bonds: The Next Generation." *Grant's Interest Rate Observer,* June 4, 2006.

Greene, Kelly. "Workers' Views on Retirement May Be Too Rosy." *Wall Street Journal,* April 4, 2006.

Gregg, Judd. "The Safety Valve Has Become a Fire Hose." *Wall Street Journal,* April 18, 2006.

Gross, Bill. "*@?#>>! Bond Trading and the Tyranny of Indexation." *PIMCO Investment Outlook,* April 2006. *www.pimco.com/LeftNav/Featured+Market+Commentary/ IO/2006/IO+April+2006.htm* (accessed October 19, 2006).

————. "As GM Goes, So Goes the Nation." *PIMCO Investment Outlook, May 2006. www.pimco.com/LeftNav/Featured+Market+Commentary/IO/2006/IO+May+2006.htm* (accessed October 19, 2006).

————. "The Strange Tale of the Bare-Bottomed King." *PIMCO Investment Outlook,* May/June 2005. *www.pimco.com/LeftNav/Featured+Market+Commentary/IO/2005/IO+May-June+2005.htm* (accessed October 19, 2006).

Gross, Daniel. "Bye-Bye, Pension!" *Slate,* January 27, 2006. *www.slate.com/id/2134931* (accessed October 19, 2006).

————. "The Cram-Down Decade." *Slate,* May 20, 2005. *www.slate.com/id/2119327* (accessed October 19, 2006).

————. "The Truth about Fannie." *Slate,* October 7, 2004. *www.slate.com/id/2107902* (accessed October 19, 2006).

————. "When Sweet Statistics Clash with a Sour Mood." *New York Times,* June 4, 2006.

————. "Why Don't Banks Fail Anymore?" *Slate,* March 27, 2006. *www.slate.com/id/2138752* (accessed October 19, 2006).

Guerrera, Francesco. "Investor Says Debt-Funded Deals Will Fuel Bankruptcies." *Financial Times* (London), June 30, 2006.

Hacker, Jacob S. *The Great Risk Shift: The Assault on American Jobs, Families, Health Care, and Retirement—And How You Can Fight Back.* New York: Oxford University Press (USA), 2006.

————. "The Privatization of Risk and the Growing Economic Insecurity of Americans." Posted February 14, 2006. *http://privatizationofrisk.ssrc.org/Hacker* (accessed October 19, 2006).

Hackney, Suzette. "More Adult Children Returning to the Nest." *Houston (TX) Chronicle,* June 18, 2006.

Hagerty, James R. "Do Countrywide's Loans Stack Up? Study of Option ARMs Sees a Performance Gap in Comparison with Rivals." *Wall Street Journal,* July 25, 2006.

———. "For-Sale Signs Multiply across U.S." *Wall Street Journal,* July 20, 2006.

———. "Millions Are Facing Monthly Squeeze on House Payments." *Wall Street Journal,* March 11, 2006.

———. "Report Decries Fannie Accounting: Data Were Manipulated to Raise Bonuses, Profit, Team Led by Rudman Finds." *Wall Street Journal,* February 24, 2006.

Hagerty, James R., and Michael Corkery. "Going, Going, Gone . . . Home Sellers Turn to Auctions in Effort to Move Properties in Slowing Housing Markets." *Wall Street Journal,* August 16, 2006.

Hagerty, James R., and Ruth Simon. "New Headache for Homeowners: Inflated Appraisals, Rosy Valuations, Common in Boom, Now Haunt Sellers. 'It's Pay-the-Piper Time'." *Wall Street Journal,* July 22, 2006.

Harney, Kenneth. "Despite Rising Rates, Homeowners Still Want to Refinance. Many Are Willing to Pay Higher Interest and Tap Their Equity for Cash." *Charlotte (NC) Observer,* August 12, 2006.

Harper, Christine. Bloomberg. "Fed's Powers May Need to Be Extended, Geithner Says." September 26, 2006.

Harper, Christine, and Jacqueline Simmons. Bloomberg. "Credit Suisse Lost $120 Million in Korean Derivatives Gone Awry." October 16, 2006.

Harrington, Shannon D., and John Glover. Bloomberg. "Credit-Default Swaps Raise Insider Trading Concerns." October 10, 2006.

Hassler, Darrell. Bloomberg. "Hedge Fund Trading of Bonds, Derivatives Doubles." September 14, 2006.

Henderson, Nell. "Fed Official Warns of Changes." *Washington Post*, March 1, 2006.

Hendrickson, David C. "The Curious Case of American Hegemony: Imperial Aspirations and National Decline." *World Policy Journal* 22, no. 2 (2005).

Hennessy-Fiske, Molly. "Private-Sector Anger Builds as Public Pension Costs Rise. Lawmakers Feel the Heat from Taxpayers Who See Their Own Benefits Wither, and Traditional Payouts Give Way to 401(k)-Style Plans." *Los Angeles Times*, October 2, 2006.

Henry, Emil. Remarks by the Treasury assistant secretary for financial institutions to the Federal Reserve Bank of Atlanta, April 18, 2006. *http://www.ustreas.gov/press/releases/js4187.htm* (accessed October 19, 2006).

Herbert, Bob. "America the Fearful." *New York Times*, May 15, 2006.

Hickey, Fred. "Anticipating the 2006–2007 Recession." *The High-Tech Strategist*, no. 225, August 2, 2006.

Henwood, Doug. "Leaking Bubble." *The Nation*, March 12, 2006.

Holtz-Eakin, Douglas. "The Economic Costs of Long-Term Federal Obligations." Testimony of the director of the Congressional Budget Office before the Committee on the Budget, U.S. Senate, February 16, 2005. *www.cbo.gov/ftpdocs/60xx/doc6094/02-16-CBO_Testimony.pdf*

Holzer, Jessica. "Hedge Fund Worry Grows. Even One Failure Could Bring About a Costly National Chain Reaction. Fund Debt Piles Up." *Houston (TX) Chronicle*, December 6, 2005.

"Home Truths: Economic Focus." *The Economist,* October 14, 2006.

Horovitz, Bruce. "Casual Dining Sites See Empty Seats: As Economy Slows, Some Consumers Eat Out Less Often." *USA Today,* July 18, 2006.

Hosking, Patrick. "Investment Banks Getting More Like Hedge Funds, Says Dr. Doom." *Times* (London), May 19, 2006.

Howley, Kathleen M. and Matthew Benjamin. Bloomberg. "Housing Slump in U.S. May Lead to First Drop since Depression." September 18, 2006.

Hudson, Michael. "Banks Gush Business Loans." *Wall Street Journal,* September 12, 2006.

———. "Many City Pension Programs Are Falling Behind, S&P Finds." *Wall Street Journal,* August 12, 2006.

Hudson, Michael, and Serena Ng. "Greenspan Expresses Concerns on Derivatives, Medicare Costs." *Wall Street Journal,* May 19, 2006.

Hulse, Carl. "Senate G.O.P. Blocks Tight Budget Rule." *New York Times,* March 14, 2006.

Humber, Yuriy. "President Supports Gold Plans." *The Moscow Times* (Russia), November 23, 2005.

Hutchinson, Martin. "The Bear's Lair: Is Japan's Past Our Future?" International Perspective, *PrudentBear.com,* July 17, 2006. *www.prudentbear.com/archive_comm_article.asp?category=International+Perspective&content_idx=56455* (accessed October 19, 2006).

————. "The Bear's Lair: Will He Be G. William Bernanke?" International Perspective, *PrudentBear.com*, July 24, 2006. *www.prudentbear.com/archive_comm_article.asp?category= International+Perspective&content_idx=56670* (accessed October 19, 2006).

"In Their Prime: Brokers, Feeling Squeezed, Are Scrambling to Serve Hedge Funds." *The Economist*, June 1, 2006.

Ip, Greg. "Fed Debate on 2000 Tech Bust Holds Lesson on Current Risks." *Wall Street Journal*, April 5, 2006.

————. "Hedge Margins Draw the Focus of Fed Official." *Wall Street Journal*, September 15, 2006.

————. "Richest Americans' Income Share Jumps Sharply." *Wall Street Journal*, September 23, 2006.

Irwin, Neil. "Is Reliance on Real Estate a Crack in the Foundation?" *Washington Post*, April 5, 2006.

————. "Our Financial Failings: Family Savings Look Scary across the Board." *Washington Post*, March 5, 2006.

"ISDA: Global Credit Derivatives Values $26T End June 2006." *Dow Jones Capital Markets Report*, September 19, 2006.

"It's All about Greed and Fear." Comstock Partners, Inc. "Daily Comment," July 12, 2006. *www.comstockfunds.com/index.cfm/ MenuItemID/164.htm* (accessed October 19, 2006).

"It's Only Just Begun: David Levy Sees Unwinding Housing Boom as Extraordinarily Destructive." Weeden & Co. LP, October 20, 2006.

Jacques, Martin. "The Death of Doha Signals the Demise of Globalisation." *The Guardian* (London), July 13, 2006.

Johnson, Steve. "Market Insight: Dollar Faces Punishment for U.S.'s Economic Imbalances." *FT.com*, April 10, 2006. *http://search.ft.com/searchArticle?queryText=steve+johnson+imbalances&y=5&javascriptEnabled=true&id=060410007467&x=13* (accessed October 19, 2006).

Jones, Steven D. "Pensions Likely to Stay Dying Breed: Law Fails to Offset Reasons for Employers to Freeze, End Defined-Benefit Programs." *Wall Street Journal*, August 29, 2006.

Jordan, Miriam. "In Immigrant Fight, Grass-Roots Groups Boost Their Clout. Internet, Talk Radio Are Used to Affect State, City Laws. Critics Slam 'Hate Groups'." *Wall Street Journal*, September 28, 2006.

Jorion, Phillipe. "Part 4: The Perceived Dangers of Following the Herd—In Recent Years, Concerns Have Been Raised that Risk Management Techniques Such as Value at Risk Could Induce Similar Trading Patterns across Banks and Thereby Increase the Volatility of Financial Markets. Are These Claims Justified?" *Financial Times* (London), September 30, 2005.

Kageyama, Uri. Associated Press. "Selling Rice to Japan? U.S. Plans to Try." March 7, 2004.

Katz, David M. "FASB Rule Puts Pensions on Balance Sheet." CFO.com, September 29, 2006. *www.cfo.com/article.cfm/7989634* (accessed October 19, 2006).

———. "Beyond Backdating: Fair-Value Fraud Risk." CFO.com, October 20, 2006. *www.cfo.com/article.cfm/8070731* (accessed October 20, 2006).

Kaufman, Henry. "How the Fed Lost Its Groove." *Wall Street Journal*, August 14, 2006.

Kempe, Frederick. "Fairy-Tale Ending May Elude Economy. Deflating Property Prices, Energy Worries, Inflation Threaten Continued Growth." *Wall Street Journal*, May 23, 2006.

————. "Why Economists Worry about Who Holds Foreign Currency Reserves." *Wall Street Journal,* May 9, 2006.

Kilbinger, Sara Seddon. "Investors, Seeking Roads to Riches, Turn to Infrastructure." *Wall Street Journal,* May 3, 2006.

Kim, Jane J. "The Credit-Card Catapult." *Wall Street Journal,* March 25, 2006.

King, Jr., Neil. "Anti-Americanism Is a Big Hit at U.N." *Wall Street Journal,* September 21, 2006.

————. "Senate Advances Foreign-Investment Legislation." *Wall Street Journal,* March 31, 2006.

Kiyosaki, Robert. "Investing: Assets That Are Lifeboats in a Shaky Future." *Yahoo! Finance,* March 7, 2006. *http://finance.yahoo .com/columnist/article/richricher/2844* (accessed October 19, 2006).

————. "Investing: Go for Gold and Silver, Not Green." *Yahoo! Finance,* March 21, 2006. *http://finance.yahoo.com/columnist/ article/richricher/2987* (accessed October 19, 2006).

Klyuev, Vladimir, and Paul Mills. "Is Housing Wealth an 'ATM'? The Relationship between Household Wealth, Home Equity Withdrawal, and Savings Rates." Working Paper WP/06/162, International Monetary Fund, June 2006. *www.imf.org/ external/pubs/ft/wp/2006/wp06162.pdf* (accessed October 19, 2006).

Knight, Jerry. "We're Stuck with the Mortgage Monsters." *Washington Post,* May 15, 2006.

Knox, Noelle. "Families Lagging in Ability to Buy Home: Ownership Rate Falls for Workers with Children." *USA Today,* March 22, 2006.

Knox, Noelle, and Mindy Fetterman. "Need to Keep House Payments Low? Try a 50-Year Mortgage." *USA Today*, May 9, 2006.

Koppel, Nathan. "Treasury to Hedge Funds: Let's Have a Little Chat about the Risks of Your Game for Everyone Else?" *Wall Street Journal*, March 11, 2006.

Kostigen, Thomas. "Derivative Danger: Somebody Should Be Worried as Loosely Regulated Market Soars." *MarketWatch*, September 26, 2006. *www.marketwatch.com/news/story/Story.aspx?guid=%7B63087831-5F18-4339-9E49-0071DBEA18F1%7D&siteid* (accessed October 19, 2006).

Kotlikoff, Laurence J. "Is the United States Bankrupt?" Federal Reserve Bank of St. Louis *Review* 88, no. 4 (2006).

Kouwe, Zachary. "Refco's Ruins." *New York Post*, April 24, 2006.

Koza, Harry. "Taxpayers Will Pay the Tab When It's 'Too Big to Fail'." *The Globe and Mail* (Toronto), August 11, 2006.

Krugman, Paul. "Debt and Denial." *New York Times*, February 18, 2006.

———. "Don't Make Nice." *New York Times*, October 23, 2006.

———. "Housing Gets Ugly." *New York Times*, August 25, 2006.

———. "Insurance Horror Stories." *New York Times*, September 22, 2006.

———. "Intimations of Recession." *New York Times*, August 7, 2006.

Lahart, Justin, and Amy Merrick. "Consumers Curb Upscale Buying as Gasoline Prices, Housing Bite." *Wall Street Journal*, August 21, 2006.

Laing, Jonathan R. "Coming Home to Roost." *Barron's*, February 13, 2006.

———. "What Could Go Wrong with China." *Barron's*, July 31, 2006.

Laperriere, Andrew. "Housing Bubble Trouble." *The Weekly Standard*, April 10, 2006.

Lauricella, Tom. "Beware the Huckster in Adviser's Clothing." *Wall Street Journal*, September 24, 2006.

Lears, Jackson. "The American Way of Debt." *New York Times*, June 11, 2006.

Leggett, Karby, Jay Solomon, and Neil King, Jr. "Threat of Wider Mideast War Grows: Israel Blames Iran, Syria for Backing Hezbollah as Fighting Escalates. Tough Choices for Washington." *Wall Street Journal*, July 14, 2006.

Lerner, Jill. "Banks at Risk: Construction Lending at Troubling Levels, FDIC Says." *Atlanta (GA) Business Chronicle*, April 2, 2006.

Lewis, Janet. "Moody's Report Slams Bank Risk Reporting: Rating Agency Argues for More and Better Disclosures and Standardization." *Investment Dealers Digest*, May 22, 2006.

Linebaugh, Kate. "Banks' Trading in Own Accounts Sifted for Conflict." *Wall Street Journal*, May 25, 2006.

Liu, Liqun, Andrew J. Rettenmaier, and Thomas R. Saving. "How Large Is the Federal Government Debt?" National Center for Policy Analysis Policy Report No. 263, October 2003. *www.ncpa.org/pub/st/st263/st263.pdf* (accessed October 19, 2006.

"Loads of Money." *The Economist*, December 23, 1999.

Lowenstein, Roger. "The End of Pensions." *New York Times*,
    October 30, 2005.

Luce, Edward. "Out on a Limb: Why Blue-Collar Americans See
    Their Future as Precarious." *Financial Times* (London), May
    3, 2006.

Lynch, David J. "Some Would Like to Build a Wall around U.S.
    Economy: Protectionism Makes a Big Comeback Grounded
    in Growing Fear, Distrust." *USA Today*, March 15, 2006.

Mandel, Michael. "Bubble, Bubble, Who's in Trouble?"
    BusinessWeek, June 15, 2006.

Mandelbrot, Benoit, and Nassim Taleb. "A Focus on the Excep-
    tions that Prove the Rule— Traditional Risk Management
    Tools Focus on What Is Normal and Consider Extreme
    Events as Ancillaries. In a World Characterised by Volatility
    and Uncertainty, Benoit Mandelbrot and Nassim Taleb Argue
    That This Approach Is Misguided, and Propose an Alterna-
    tive Methodology Where Large Deviations Dominate the
    Analysis." *Financial Times* (London), March 24, 2006.

Maranjian, Selena. "Are You Ready for Disaster?" *Motley Fool*,
    March 29, 2006. *www.fool.com/news/mft/2006/mft06032906
    .htm* (accessed October 19, 2006).

Mayer, Martin. "Risk Reduction in the New Financial
    Architecture: Realities, Fallacies, and Proposals." Working
    Paper 268, The Levy Economics Institute of Bard College,
    Annandale-on-Hudson, NY, April 1999. *http://papers.ssrn.com/
    sol3/Delivery.cfm/99052003.pdf?abstractid=165550&mirid=1*
    (accessed October 19, 2006).

McBride, Sarah. "How Do You Get a Break in the Price of
    Practically Anything? Easy, Just Ask." *Wall Street Journal*,
    August 19, 2006.

McConnell, Bill. "The Return of 'Too Big to Fail'." *TheDeal.com*, October 7, 2005. *www.thedeal.com*.

McCutcheon, Chuck. "Experts Warn U.S. Is Coming Apart at the Seams." *The Seattle (WA) Times*, August 26, 2006.

McDonald, Ian, Kate Linebaugh, and Andrew Morse. "Surviving a Market's Ups and Downs—Playing the Falling-Dollar Game: Overseas Holdings Get a Boost but Currency Bets Can Be Risky." *Wall Street Journal*, May 20, 2006.

McLean, Bethany. "The Mystery of the $890 Billion Insurer: MBIA Guarantees the Safety of Bonds That Fund Everything from the Eurotunnel to Commercial Aircraft to Cities across America. A Relentless Short-Seller Charges That Its Business Model Isn't Sound. Can He Be Right?" *Fortune*, May 16, 2005.

McMahon, E. J. "Public Pension Price Tag." *Wall Street Journal*, August 21, 2006.

McQueen, M. P. "Health Insurers Must Cover Adult Children." *Wall Street Journal*, April 11, 2006.

Merton, Robert K. *Social Theory and Social Structure.* New York: Free Press, 1968.

Michael, Clarence. "Greenback Vulnerable to Reshuffle of Gulf State Coffers." *Business Times*, April 7, 2006.

Miller, Leslie, Associated Press. "Foreign Companies Buy U.S. Roads, Bridges." July 15, 2006.

Mills, Elinor. "Reich: U.S. Headed for 'Day of Reckoning'." *CNET News.com*, March 8, 2006. *http://news.com.com/Reich+U.S.+ headed+for+day+of+reckoning/2100-1022_3-6047237.html* (accessed October 19, 2006).

Mollenkamp, Carrick. "Tracing Refco's Ruin Leads Probe to Bermuda." *Wall Street Journal*, March 30, 2006.

Mollenkamp, Carrick, and Charles Fleming. "Why Students of Prof. El Karoui Are in Demand." *Wall Street Journal*, March 9, 2006.

Mollenkamp, Carrick, Ian McDonald, and Peter A. McKay. "Behind Big Wall Street Failure: An Unregulated Bermuda Unit. Court Proceedings Help Show How Refco Hid Bad Debt, Planning Project 'Cleanup,' The Missing $1.8 Billion." *Wall Street Journal*, July 3, 2006.

Murray, Alan. "Voters' Doubts About Sharing in Prosperity Send a Danger Signal." *Wall Street Journal*, October 25, 2006.

Mysak, Joe. Bloomberg. "$1 Trillion Shock Awaits States, Local Governments." June 30, 2006.

———. Bloomberg. "It's Time to Come Clean on Muni Swaps, Derivatives." June 14, 2006.

"The New Bankruptcy Law." FindLaw for the Public. *http://bankruptcy.findlaw.com/new-bankruptcy-law* (accessed October 19, 2006).

Newman, Barry. "Employers Have a Lot to Lose." *Wall Street Journal*, April 11, 2006.

New York Times editorial. "Downward Mobility." August 30, 2006.

New York Times editorial. "Who Bears the Risk?" September 17, 2006.

Ng, Serena. "Easy Money? Banks Get Lenient on Loans." *Wall Street Journal*, April 7, 2006.

Nicolaci da Costa, Pedro. Reuters. "Wall Street Touts Transparency, Yearns for Secrecy." May 30, 2005.

Norris, Floyd. "Are These Hedge Fund Results Real?" *New York Times*, April 21, 2006.

————. "From Buffett, Folksy Talk about Losing Serious Money." *New York Times*, March 6, 2006.

————. "Options Brought Riches and Now Big Trouble." *New York Times*, July 25, 2006.

"Now for the Reckoning: Corporate America's Legacy Costs." *The Economist*, October 15, 2006.

Nutting, Rex. "Lenders Gone Wild: Can U.S. Curb the 'Exotic Mortgages' Frenzy That Puts Homeowners at Risk?" *MarketWatch*, September 29, 2006. *www.marketwatch.com/news/story/Story.aspx?guid=%7BD65CBE06-491D-437F-B9F8-851F37D 54B39%7D&siteid=mktw* (accessed October 19, 2006).

————. "Recession Will Be Nasty and Deep, Economist Says. Housing Is in Free Fall, Pulling the Economy Down with It, Roubini Argues." *MarketWatch*, August 23, 2006. *www.marketwatch.com/News/Story/Story.aspx?dist=newsfinder &siteid=mktw&guid=%7BE18E95AF-DBFF-4EE4-ACF7 -530A3CD714D3%7D&symbol* (accessed October 19, 2006).

————. "U.S. Household Debt Up Most in 20 Years." *MarketWatch*, March 9, 2006. *www.marketwatch.com/News/Story/ Story.aspx?guid=%7B1E78F574-16D7-46AE-8D23-EC479D355 E02%7D&dist=newsfinder&siteid=mktw&keyword=* (accessed October 19, 2006).

Oakley, David. "Bond Protections Not Reliable—Fitch." *FT.com*, October 18, 2006. *www.ft.com/cms/s/54e490d0-5ede-11db -afac-0000779e2340.html* (accessed October 19, 2006).

"OCC Bank Derivatives Report: Second Quarter 2006." Office of the Comptroller of the Currency.

Paletta, Damian. "Regulator Warns of Lending Risk in Property Sector." *Wall Street Journal*, October 6, 2006.

Panzner, Michael J. "The Coming Disaster in the Derivatives Market." *Financial Sense Online*, November 9, 2005. *www.financialsense.com/editorials/2005/1109_b.html* (accessed October 19, 2006).

———. *The New Laws of the Stock Market Jungle: An Insider's Guide to Successful Investing in a Changing World.* Upper Saddle River, NJ: *Financial Times* Prentice Hall, 2004.

Pardomuan, Lewa. Reuters. "China's Gold Reserves 'Too Low,' May Buy on Price Dip." August 31, 2006.

Parker, George. "Europe Simulates Financial Meltdown." *FT.com*, April 9, 2006. *http://search.ft.com/searchArticle?queryText= europe+simulates+financial+meltdown&y=7&javascriptEnabled= true&id=060409003558&x=17* (accessed October 19, 2006).

Parkinson, Patrick M. Testimony of the deputy director of the Division of Research and Statistics of the Federal Reserve Board before the Subcommittee on Securities and Investment, Committee on Banking, Housing, and Urban Affairs, U.S. Senate, May 16, 2006. *www.federalreserve.gov/ boarddocs/testimony/2006/20060516/default.htm* (accessed October 19, 2006).

Partnoy, Frank, and David Skeel. "Credit Derivatives Play a Dangerous Game." *Financial Times* (London), July 17, 2006.

Honorable Ron Paul of Texas. "Why Are Americans So Angry?" Speech before the U.S. House of Representatives, June 29, 2006. *www.house.gov/paul/congrec/congrec2006/cr062906.htm* (accessed October 19, 2006).

Pennacchi, George. "Deposit Insurance, Bank Regulation, and Financial System Risks." Center for Financial Research, FDIC, Working Paper, presented at the Conference on Financial Innovation, Risk, and Fragility, April 15–16, 2005. Published August 2005. *www.fdic.gov/bank/analytical/cfr/2005/sept/ cfrfall_2005_Pennacchi.pdf* (accessed October 19, 2006).

"Pension Crash Landing." *Wall Street Journal*, June 27, 2006.

"The Pension Era, R.I.P." *Wall Street Journal*, August 4, 2006.

Plender, John. "The Credit Business Is More Perilous Than Ever." *Financial Times* (London), October 13, 2006.

Porter, Eduardo. "If Detroit Calls, U.S. May Not Replay the Bailout Role." *New York Times*, April 14, 2006.

Porterfield, Bob, Associated Press. "Retiree Health Care May Overwhelm Governments." September 24, 2006.

Postman, David. "Gingrich Says It's World War III." *Seattle (WA) Times*, July 15, 2006.

Powell, Bob. "The Oil Shocks of the '70s." Posted May 4, 2005. *www.exponentialimprovement.com/cms/oilshock.shtml* (accessed October 19, 2006).

Powell, Eileen Alt, Associated Press. "Consumers Find It Harder to Keep Up with Their Debt: Higher Interest Rates, Gas Prices Leave Many Feeling Like They're Drowning in Debt." July 5, 2006.

Prechter, Robert. "Popular Culture and the Stock Market." *Elliott Wave Theorist*, August 1985. *www.socionomics.net/PDF/popular_culture.pdf* (accessed October 19, 2006).

PRNewswire. "U.S. Sovereign Ratings Could Be Undermined by L-T Age-Related Spending Trends, Says S&P Report." June 6, 2006.

Pulliam, Susan. "The Hedge-Fund King Is Getting Nervous: Inside Billionaire Steve Cohen's Hidden World of Massive Trading and Lavish Art. Is the Party Over?" *Wall Street Journal*, September 16, 2006.

Quarles, Randal K. Remarks of the Under Secretary of the Treasury for Domestic Finance to the Global Association of Risk Professionals, March 1, 2006. *www.ustreas.gov/press/releases/js4081.htm* (accessed October 19, 2006).

————. Remarks of the Under Secretary of the Treasury for Domestic Finance to the National Association of State Treasurers, March 6, 2006. *www.ustreas.gov/press/releases/js4094.htm* (accessed October 19, 2006).

Rafferty, Kevin. "A Dangerous Empire of U.S. Debt." *The Standard* (Hong Kong), February 17, 2006.

Ramstack, Tom. "Energy Costs Shock Budgets." *Washington (D.C.) Times*, March 10, 2006.

Rapoport, Michael. "Hedge Accounting Gets on Regulators' Radar." *Wall Street Journal*, January 27, 2006.

Reagor, Catherine. "Risky ARM Mortgages Come Due." *Arizona Republic*, May 5, 2006.

Reason, Tim. "Securitization: Cash Flow on Tap. A Popular Financing Technique, Sometimes Criticized for Its Off-Balance-Sheet Treatment, May Be Skewing Cash-Flow Statement Too, Says a New Report." CFO.com, June 30, 2006. *www.cfo.com/article.cfm/7108117?f=search* (accessed October 19, 2006).

Reilly, David. "FASB to Move Pension Accounting from Footnotes to Balance Sheets." *Wall Street Journal*, March 31, 2006.

Reuters. "Americans Keep Snapping Up Second Homes." April 6, 2006.

Reuters. "Fed's Bies Cites Concern at U.S. Banks' Commercial Lending." October 11, 2006.

Reuters. "Fed's Geithner Says Wary of Derivatives Risks."
February 28, 2006.

Reuters. "Homebuilder Confidence Hits 15-Year Low."
September 18, 2006.

Reuters. "NY Fed Head Sees Benefits, Risks in Derivatives."
May 16, 2006.

Reuters. "Sharpe Ratio, Key Hedge Fund Risk Gauge 'Flawed'."
July 23, 2006.

Reuters. "Some Hedge Funds May Pose Stability Risk." January
25, 2006.

Reuters. "Study: CEOs Expect Declining Economic Growth. A
Survey By Business Roundtable Shows Chief Execs at Large
Companies Wary of Slowdown." September 18, 2006.

Reuters. "U.S. Mortgage Bonds Face Risk If House Prices Fall-
BIS." March 5, 2006.

Richard, Christine. "MBIA's Bond Exposure Increases Junk
Debt—Business Triples as Reinsurers' Ratings Fall, Squeezing
Capital Cushion." *Wall Street Journal*, October 29, 2003.

Richard, Christine. Bloomberg. "Pension Deficit, Now $500
Billion, May Clobber Corporate Bonds." May 16, 2006.

Risk, Hamish. Bloomberg. "Credit Derivatives Led by Too Few
Banks, Fitch Says." November 18, 2005.

Robb, Greg. "Storm Clouds Seen over Markets: IMF."
MarketWatch, April 11, 2006 *www.marketwatch.com/News/Story/
Story.aspx?guid=%7B7F74606B-DD80-44A4-B5B8-047C6D5D42
E1%7D&siteid=mktw&dist=* (accessed October 19, 2006).

Rogers, David. "House Passes Border-Fence Bill, Changes to
Rules on Earmarks." *Wall Street Journal*, September 15, 2006.

Rolnick, Arthur J. "Deposit Insurance Reform: Market Discipline as a Regulator of Bank Risk." *http://minneapolisfed.org/research/studies/tbtf/market.cfm* (accessed October 19, 2006).

Rosenberg, Yuval. "The Boomer Bust." *Fortune,* June 19, 2006.

Rose, J. S. et al, eds. *Multivariate Applications in Substance Use Research: New Methods for New Questions.* Mahwah, NJ: LEA, Inc., 1979.

Ruffenach, Glenn. "Many Households Are at Risk in Their Retirement Finances." *Wall Street Journal,* June 6, 2006.

Ryan, Jennifer, and Hamish Risk. Bloomberg. "Credit-Default Swap Market Whipsawed by Verizon, Rentokil Debt." August 8, 2006.

Sahadi, Jeanne. "Social Security, Medicare to Run Out Soon." *CNNMoney.com,* May 1, 2006. *http://money.cnn.com/2006/05/01/retirement/SStrustees_2006report/index.htm* (accessed October 19, 2006).

————. "Tick. Tick. Beware the Mortgage Time-Bomb." *CNNMoney.com,* October 9, 2006. *http://money.cnn.com/2006/10/09/real_estate/arms_nightmare/index.htm* (accessed October 19, 2006).

Saha-Bubna, Aparajita. "Ruling Shakes Up Hybrid Securities." *Wall Street Journal,* March 21, 2006.

Salas, Caroline. Bloomberg. "Hybrid Bond Market Grinds to a 'Halt' after Ruling on Lehman." April 26, 2006.

Saletan, William. "Curse of the Young Old: Why Should We Pay Them?" *Washington Post,* March 19, 2006.

Samuelson, Robert J. "A Financial 'Time Bomb'?" *Washington Post,* March 12, 2003.

Saunders, Jim. "Florida Gives Insurance Firms a Helping Hand." *Daytona Beach (FL) News-Journal,* May 17, 2006.

Schaefer, Standard. "An Interview with Economist Michael Hudson: The Coming Financial Reality." *CounterPunch,* July 11, 2003. *www.counterpunch.org/schaefer07122003.html* (accessed October 19, 2006.

Schifferes, Steve. "The End of the American Dream?" *BBC News,* September 4, 2006. *http://news.bbc.co.uk/go/pr/fr/-/2/hi/ business/5303590.stm* (accessed October 19, 2006).

Schoen, John W. "Why Is the National Debt Out of Control?" *MSNBC.com,* September 29, 2006. *www.msnbc.msn.com/ id/15064460* (accessed October 19, 2006).

Scholtes, Saskia. "A Spectacular Parting of the Ways." *Financial Times* (London), August 22, 2006.

Schroeder, Michael. "Massive Hurricane Claims Force U.S. Flood Insurance Overhaul." *Wall Street Journal,* January 26, 2006.

Schroeder, Robert. "Treasury Studying Market Impact of Derivatives, Hedge Funds." *MarketWatch,* March 13, 2006. *www.marketwatch.com/News/Story/Story.aspx?siteid=mktw&guid= %7B0EB7B26F-0A14-4855-A4C7-83398824DA54%7D* (accessed October 19, 2006).

Schultz, Ellen E., Charles Forelle, and Theo Francis. "Forecast: More Pension Freezes." *Wall Street Journal,* January 12, 2006.

Schultz, Ellen E., and Theo Francis. "How Safe Is Your Pension?" *Wall Street Journal,* January 12, 2006.

Scott, Peter Dale, Pacific News Service. "Homeland Security Contracts for Vast New Detention Camps." February 8, 2006.

Sender, Henny. "The Betting on GM." *Wall Street Journal,* November 25, 2005.

————. "A Company's Road to Restructuring May Teem with Hedge-Fund Potholes." *Wall Street Journal,* March 30, 2006.

————. "Concerns Dog Credit Derivatives." *Wall Street Journal,* March 1, 2006.

————. "Debt Buyers vs. The Indebted: Showdown Between Hedge Funds and Private Equity May Be Inevitable." *Wall Street Journal,* October 17, 2006.

Sesit, Michael. Bloomberg. "Smithers Sees Earnings Worldwide Peaking, Undermining Stocks." July 10, 2006.

Shaw, Helen. "Pensions, Leases Worry PCAOB Member." CFO.com, September 12, 2006. *www.cfo.com/article.cfm/7904533* (accessed October 19, 2006).

Shearmur, Malcolm. Bloomberg. "Swiss State Pension Fund Plans to Sell U.S. Bonds on Debt Worry." November 7, 2005.

Shedlock, Michael. "Baby Boomer Time Bombs." Mish's Global Economic Trend Analysis, January 5, 2006 blog entry. *http://globaleconomicanalysis.blogspot.com/2006_01_05_ globaleconomicanalysis_archive.html* (accessed October 19, 2006).

Shenn, Jody. "A Mortgage Bond 'Shock' Called Likely." *American Banker Online,* August 10, 2006. *www.americanbanker.com/ article_search.html?articlequeryid=909743337&hitnum=47* (accessed October 19, 2006).

Shilling, A. Gary. "End of the Bubble Bailouts." *Forbes.com,* August 29, 2006. *www.forbes.com/investmentnewsletters/2006/08/28/ housing-crash-bubble-in_ags_0828soapbox_inl.html* (accessed October 19, 2006).

Silver, Vernon, and Otis Bilodeau. Bloomberg. "Refco Bank Hid $1 Billion Loss from Hedge Funds, Arafat Casino." June 22, 2006.

Silverblatt, Howard. "America's Other Pension Problem." *BusinessWeek*, December 19, 2005.

Silverman, Rachel Emma. "A Fortress for Your Money: How to Guard Against Lawsuits and Other Claims on Assets. The 'Equity Strip' Maneuver." *Wall Street Journal*, July 15, 2006.

Simmons, Jacqueline. "Derivatives Dynamo." *Bloomberg Markets*, January 2006.

Simon, Ruth. "More Home Loans Go Sour. Though New Data Show Rising Delinquencies, Lenders Continue to Loosen Mortgage Standards." *Wall Street Journal*, October 19, 2006.

Sloan, Allan. "D.C.'s Deficit Math Doesn't Add Up." *Newsweek*, September 18, 2006.

Smith, George F. "Season's Greetings from the Fed." Strike the Root, December 29, 2004 blog entry. *www.strike-the-root.com/4/smith/smith12.html* (accessed October 19, 2006).

"So Long Footnoted Liabilities." *CFO Magazine*, February 1, 2006.

Solomon, Deborah, and James R. Hagerty. "White House Weighs Move to Rein in Fannie and Freddie. Treasury Threatens to Use Its Power on Debt Issuance If Congress Doesn't Act." *Wall Street Journal*, June 14, 2006.

Solomon, Deborah, and Lee Hawkins, Jr. "Pension Inquiry Shines Spotlight on Assumptions. Small Changes in Calculations at Companies Have a Big Effect on Retiree Liability—and Profit." *Wall Street Journal*, November 9, 2005.

Sprague, Irvine H. *Bailout: An Insider's Account of Bank Failures and Rescues*. New York: Basic Books, 1986.

Springen, Karen. "Going For Broke: Elizabeth Warren Discusses How Ordinary Families Wind Up Bankrupt and Why New Legislation Could Be Hurting Those at Risk." *Newsweek*, August 31, 2006, *www.msnbc.msn.com/id/14604090/site/newsweek/* (accessed October 19, 2006).

Sterman, John. *Business Dynamics: Systems Thinking for a Complex World* (Instructors Manual). New York: McGraw-Hill/Irwin, 2000.

Stevenson, Richard W. "In Only 4 Months, Greenspan Changes Economic Tune." *New York Times*, October 8, 1998.

Stewart, Heather. "U.S.-China Trade War Looms." *The Observer* (London), March 26, 2006.

Steyn, Mark. "It's the Demography, Stupid: The Real Reason the West Is in Danger of Extinction." *Wall Street Journal Online*, January 4, 2006. *www.opinionjournal.com/extra/?id=110007760* (accessed October 19, 2006).

Stone, Amey. "The Great Depression vs. the Millennial Slowdown." *BusinessWeek Online*, August 20, 2001. *www.businessweek.com/bwdaily/dnflash/aug2001/nf20010820_857.htm* (accessed October 19, 2006).

Streitfeld, David. "More Home Buyers Stretch Truth, Budgets to Get Loans. As Southland Housing Cools Off, Reports of Fraud Grow, Raising Fears of a Wave of Foreclosures." *Los Angeles Times*, September 29, 2006.

Strohecker, Alister. Reuters. "More Countries Could Develop Nuclear Bombs: IAEA." October 16, 2006.

"Super Scandal: Congress Ignores Threat to Banking System." *San Diego (CA) Union-Tribune*, July 10, 2006.

Swann, Christopher. "Housing Boom Will Not End in a Crash, Says Harvard." *Financial Times* (London), June 13, 2006.

Szala, Ginger, and James T. Holter. "In the Mood, or How to Profit from Socionomics." *Futures,* November 2004.

Taub, Stephen. "Fannie Mae Finds $10.8B in Errors." *CFO. com,* November 10, 2005. *www.cfo.com/article.cfm/5154885* (accessed October 19, 2006).

———. "First Data Restates Over Derivatives." *CFO.com,* August 23, 2006. *www.cfo.com/article.cfm/7826906* (accessed October 19, 2006).

———. "MBIA to Restate Seven Years of Results. This Is the Second Major Insurer This Year to Revise Its Financials Due to Accounting for Complex Reinsurance Agreements, and More Companies May Follow." *CFO.com,* March 9, 2005. *www.cfo.com/ article.cfm/3738637* (accessed October 19, 2006).

———. "Moody's Cites Effects of New Pension Law." *CFO.com,* August 18, 2006. *www.cfo.com/article.cfm/7814329* (accessed October 19, 2006).

Terhune, Chad, and Theo Francis, "Hurricanes Squeeze Insurers of Last Resort." *Wall Street Journal,* October 24, 2005.

Tett, Gillian. "Derivatives Activity Linked to Share Falls." *Financial Times* (London), May 19, 2006.

———. "Prime Brokers Selling Hedge Fund Exposure Marks Watershed." *Financial Times* (London), June 23, 2006.

Thornton, Emily, David Henry, and Adrienne Carter. "Inside Wall Street's Culture of Risk." *BusinessWeek,* June 12, 2006.

Thornton, Philip. "IMF: Risk of Global Crash Is Increasing." *The Independent* (London), September 13, 2006.

Thurow, Roger. "For Hungry Kids, 'Backpack Clubs' Try to Fill the Gap." *Wall Street Journal,* June 14, 2006.

Torres, Craig, and Alexandre Tanzi. Bloomberg. "'Hourglass Economy Divides Americans, Defines U.S. Politics." August 3, 2006.

"Toward Greater Financial Stability: A Private Sector Perspective." Report of the Counterparty Risk Management Policy Group II, July 27, 2005. *www.crmpolicygroup.org/docs/ CRMPG-II.pdf* (accessed October 19, 2006).

"Trading Shots: Are Derivatives Weapons of Mass Financial Destruction? Is a Meltdown Cooking in Exotic Assets, or Can Markets Handle the Next LTCM?" *Wall Street Journal Online,* May 5, 2006. *http://online.wsj.com/PA2VJBNA4R/article/ SB114675328154243771-search. http://online.wsj.com/ PA2VJBNA4R/article/SB114675328154243771-search .html?KEYWORDS= trading+shots+derivatives&COLLECTION = wsjie/6month* (accessed October 19, 2006).

Trahant, Mark. "Today's Bust Is All about Credit." *Seattle (WA) Post-Intelligencer,* September 17, 2006.

Trumbull, Mark. "Why Budget Fixes Can't Wait: Rising Longevity, Health Care Costs, and Federal Obligations Will Force a Reckoning in the U.S., Experts Say." *Christian Science Monitor,* January 10, 2006.

"Two-Thirds of Lenders Nationwide Say U.S. in Midst of Real Estate Bubble—and Half Say Burst Has Begun or Will Shortly, According to Phoenix Lending Survey Results." Phoenix Management Services, Chadds Ford, PA. April 4, 2006. *www.phoenixmanagement.com/newsroom/two-thirds-of- lenders-nationwide-say-us-in-midst-of-real-estate-bubble-and-half-say- burst-has-begun-or-will-shortly-according-to-phoenix-lending-survey- results* (accessed October 19, 2006).

Tyson, James L. Bloomberg. "Fannie Mae, Freddie Mac Retreat as Mortgage Bond Market Mutates." September 6, 2006.

————. "Fannie Mae's Mudd, Unfazed by Probes, Will Buy Riskier Loans." May 5, 2006.

Ullman, Harlan. "America Gone Bad." *Washington (D.C.) Times,* June 20, 2006.

Webb-Vidal, Andy. "Bush Told to Plan for Chavez Oil Shock." *Financial Times* (London), July 24, 2006.

Waddington, Richard, and William Schomberg. Reuters. "World Trade Talks Collapse." July 24, 2006.

Waggoner, John. "How Long Can Households Sustain Negative Savings?" *USA Today,* March 2, 2006.

————. "How to Hedge against Two Scary Scenarios." *USA Today,* July 1, 2005.

"Waking the Dogs: Financial Markets Have Been Eerily Calm for Most of the Past Two Years. No Longer." *The Economist,* November 1, 1005.

Honorable David M. Walker. "Saving Our Future Requires Tough Choices Today." Speech of the Comptroller General of the United States at the University of Texas, Austin, Texas, September 28, 2006. *www.gao.gov/cghome/d061138cg.pdf* (accessed October 19, 2006).

Wallison, Peter J. "1.5 Trillion of Debt." *Wall Street Journal,* March 7, 2006.

Walsh, Mary Williams. "More Companies Ending Promises for Retirement." *New York Times,* January 9, 2006.

————. "Public Pension Plans Face Billions in Shortages." *New York Times,* August 8, 2006.

————. "Shocks Seen in New Math for Pensions." *New York Times,* March 31, 2006.

Walter, John R., and John A. Weinberg. "How Large Is the Federal Financial Safety Net?" *Cato Journal* 21, no. 3 (2002).

Ward, Sandra. "Awash in a Sea of Debt." *Barron's*, July 24, 2006.

———. "Beware the Spent Consumer." *Barron's*, June 5, 2006.

———. "Signs of the Bear." *Barron's*, July 3, 2006.

Wasik, John. Bloomberg. "S&P 500 May Drop If Full Pension Debts Disclosed." December 5, 2005.

Wei, Lingling. "'Stated Income Home Mortgages Raise Red Flags." *Wall Street Journal*, August 22, 2006.

Weinberg, Neil, and Nathan Vardi. "Private Inequity: The Mad Rush into Private Equity—Is Your Retirement at Risk?" *Forbes*, March 13, 2006.

Wessell, David. "How Will the U.S. Fill Its Benefits Gap?" *Wall Street Journal*, April 13, 2006.

———. "How Would Hedge Funds Behave in a Crisis?" *Wall Street Journal*, July 20, 2006.

———. "To a Seer, It's Clear: Budget Will Buckle under Health Costs," *Wall Street Journal*, January 12, 2006.

———. "U.S. Wages Face Glut of Pressures." *Wall Street Journal*, June 15, 2006.

Weston, Liz Pulliam. "The Truth about Social Security Is Ugly." MSN Money. *http://moneycentral.msn.com/content/RetirementandWills/P77627.asp* (accessed October 19, 2006).

Whalen, Christopher. "A New Form for Risk: Are These Derivatives Over-the-Counter, or Under It?" *Barron's*, June 5, 3006.

"What a Social Downtrend Looks & Feels Like." Elliott Wave International, June 8, 2006. *www.elliottwave.com/features/default.aspx?cat=pmp&aid=2445* (accessed October 19, 2006).

Whitehouse, Mark. "Slices of Risk: How a Formula Ignited Market That Burned Some Big Investors. Credit Derivatives Got a Boost from Clever Pricing Model, Hedge Funds Misused It. Inspiration, Widowed Spouses." *Wall Street Journal,* September 12, 2005.

———. "U.S. Foreign Debt Shows Its Teeth as Rates Climb. Net Payments Remain Small but Pose Long-Term Threat to Nation's Living Standards." *Wall Street Journal,* September 25, 2006.

Whitehouse, Mark, and Craig Karmin. "Markets Brace for Japan's Shift on Monetary Policy." *Wall Street Journal,* March 1, 2006.

Whitehouse, Mark, and Gregory Zuckerman. "Housing Bears Bet on Shaky Credit." *Wall Street Journal,* December 12, 2005.

Wigan, David. Reuters. "Credit Derivative Errors Soar in 2005-ISDA." May 30, 2006.

———. "IMF Warns Over Credit Derivative Liquidity," April 11, 2006.

Wighton, David. "Investment Banks Increase Their Exposure to Buy-Outs." *FT.com,* July 16, 2006. *http://search.ft.com/search Article?queryText=investment+banks+wighton&javascriptEnabled=true&id=060716003627* (accessed October 19, 2006).

Wilde, Gerald J. S. *Target Risk.* Toronto, Ont.: PDE Publications, 1994.

Will, George F. "Guaranteed Collisions." *Washington Post,* May 15, 2005.

Willett, Brady, and Todd Always. "The Long-Term Consequences of the Long-Term Bailout." *Fallstreet.com,* August 16, 2006. *www.fallstreet.com/aug1606.php* (accessed October 19, 2006).

Wines, Michael. "How Bad Is Inflation in Zimbabwe?" *New York Times,* May 2, 2006.

Witter, Lon. "The No-Money-Down Disaster." *Barron's,* August 21, 2006.

Wolf, Martin. "Dangers of the Housing Market Delusion," *Financial Times* (London), April 17, 2006.

———. "A Slowing U.S. Could Brake the World." *Financial Times* (London), September 26, 2006.

Wolf, Richard. "As Social Security Surges and Medicare Takes Off, the Deficit Will Soar. The Result: 'Fiscal Hurricane.' Economists Say Unchecked Spending Will Trigger Recessions and Worse." *USA Today,* November 15, 2005.

Wolk, Martin. "Cost of Iraq War Could Surpass $1 Trillion. Estimates Vary, but All Agree Price Is Far Higher Than Initially Expected." *MSNBC.com,* March 17, 2006. *http://msnbc.msn.com/id/11880954* (accessed October 19, 2006).

———. "How a Housing Downturn Could Roil Economy." MSNBC.com, March 3, 2006. *http://msnbc.msn.com/id/11658208* (accessed October 19, 2006).

Woodall, Pam. "The Unfinished Recession: Obituaries for the Business Cycle Were Premature. Indeed, Economies Could Become More Volatile Again over the Coming Years, Argues Pam Woodall, Our Economics Editor." *The Economist,* September 26, 2002.

Woodyard, Chris. "For Many Car Hunters Today, Leasing's the Way to Go." *USA Today,* April 5, 2006.

"World Finance: The Coming Storm for Banks." *The Economist,* February 20, 2004.

Wright, Tom. "Trade Focus Now Shifts to Regional Deals." *New York Times,* July 26, 2006.

Wright, Tom, and Steven R. Weisman. "Trade Talks Fail over an Impasse on Farm Tariffs." *New York Times,* July 25, 2006.

Wysocki, Jr., Bernard. "Bankers and Regulators Clash over Surge in Real-Estate Loans." *Wall Street Journal,* September 11, 2006.

Wysocki, Jr., Bernard, and Aaron Lucchetti. "Global Exchanges Pose a Quandary for Securities Cops. Nymex's Squabble with Rival over U.K. Rules Spotlights Issues for NYSE Merger." *Wall Street Journal,* June 5, 2006.

Yao, Deborah. "Device Offers Detour around Bad Credit: Users Can't Start Car If They Don't Make Payment on Time." *Houston (TX) Chronicle,* June 19, 2006.

Yao, Kevin, and Benjamin Kang Lim. Reuters. "Senior China Official Urges Cut in U.S. Debt Holding." April 4, 2006.

Zuckerman, Gregory. "Companies on a Borrowing Binge: Can They Handle All the Debt? Whether Excessive or Not, It May Hurt Bonds, Help Stocks." *Wall Street Journal,* August 17, 2006.

Zuckerman, Gregory, and Scott Patterson. "'Side-Pocket' Accounts of Hedge Funds Studied." *Wall Street Journal,* August 4, 2006.

INDEX